I Paved the Way for Real Divas: Selected Classical Singers, Composers & Pianists

Arthur Petersen

Arthur Petersen

I Paved the Way for Real Divas: Selected Classical Singers, Composers & Pianists ©2023 by Arthur Petersen
All Rights Reserved.
No part of this book may be reproduced in any form without written permission from the publisher.

Published by:
BTB PUBLISHING LLC
New York

ISBN: 978-1-63652-115-2

I Paved the Way for Real Divas: Selected Classical Singers, Composers & Pianists

Arthur Petersen

Arthur Petersen

Arthur Petersen, indigenous of Christiansted, Virgin Islands (VI), was reared by his grandparents, Edna Thomas Petersen, and Pierpont Alexander Petersen. A product of the VI Public Schools, graduating from Saint Croix Central High School in 1989.

Petersen graduated from Clinton College in Rock Hill, South Carolina, and has worked at Lew Muckle Elementary School in Sion Farm for 20 years. He has traveled to the Republic of Cuba, the Kingdom of Morocco, the Portuguese Republic, and Spain, and extensively throughout the eastern corridor of the United States.

Petersen is the author of *Quiet Quotes in 4 Seasons*. His work has also appeared in *Second Coming or Second Trade-off: Contemporary & Relevant Literature during the Pandemic*.

TABLE OF CONTENTS

Dedication
Acknowledgments

Introduction, 12

Part I: **SINGERS**, 14

Joaquina Maria da Conceição Lapinha (1785-1812), 14

Elizabeth Greenfield Taylor (1809-1976), 16

Matilda Sissieretta Joyner/Madame Jones (1869-1933), 18

Florence Cole-Talbert McCleave (1890-1961), 20

Caterina Jarboro (1896-1986), 23

Marian Anderson (1897-1993), 26

Aisha Musa Ahmad (1905-1974), 30

Dorothy Leigh Maynor (1910-1996), 32

Camilla Ella Williams (1919-2012), 35

Charlotte Wesley Holloman (1922-2015), 39

Muriel Burrell Smith (1923-1985), 42

Arthur Petersen

Mattiwilda Dobbs (1925-2015), 44

Adele Addison Berger (1925-), 47

Mary Leontyne Price (1927-), 49

Gloria Davy (1931-2012), 51

Shirley Verrett (1931-2010), 53

Ella Ruth Lee (1933-2013), 55

Martina Arroyo (1937-), 57

Grace Melzia Bumbry (1937-2010), 60

Jessye Norman (1945-2019), 63

Kathleen Deanna Battle (1948-), 66

Lorraine Elizabeth Baa (1953-2021), 68

Monica Nieves Jacobs (1956-), 71

Ingrid A. Bough (1959-), 73

Denyce Graves (1964-), 75

Audra Ann McDonald (1970-), 77

Elizabeth Caballero (1974-), 80

Diamela del Pozo Pérez (1976-), 83

Pumeza Matshikiza (1979-), 85

Omo Bello (1982-), 87

I Paved the Way

Onika Michelle Thomas (1984-), 89

Angel Joy Blue (1984-), 91

Pretty Yende (1985-), 93

J'Nai Bridges (1987), 95

Yolisa Ngwexana, 97

Khayakazi Madlala, 99

Other Up and coming South African Opera Singers, 101

Part II: **PIANISTS**, 102

Catalina Berroa Ojea (1849-1911), 102

Carmen Velma Shepperd (1910-1997), 104

Sylvia Olden Lee (1917 –2004), 107

Hazel Dorothy Scott (1920-1981), 110

Helen I. Francis Joseph (1921-2020), 113

Jeanette Hayslett Wallace (1930-2017), 115

Nina Simone (1933-2003), 117

Geraldine Hayslett Thomas Boone (1936-), 121

Phyllis King Leach, 123

Hildred Elizabeth Roach (1937-), 125
Philippa Smith Tyler (1946-), 127

Adele Darlene Allen (1953-), 129

Barbara-Gene Forde Browne (1956-), 132

Paula Harrell, 135

Part III: COMPOSERS, 138

Florence Beatrice Smith Price (1887-1953), 138

Undine Smith Moore (1904-1989), 140

Tania Justina León (1945-), 143

Nkeiru Okoye (1972-), 145

SELECTED MUSIC PROGRAMS, 148

SELECTED OPERA HOUSES IN YOUR AREA, 151

NOTES, 154

BIBLIOGRAPHY, 165

Dedication

In 2021, during the middle of the COVID-19 Pandemic, I had the opportunity to substitute in music at Lew Muckle Elementary School in Sion Farm, St. Croix; during this period, I began reading about the lives of musicians and listening to some of the great music that they produced as a performer and composer. I was thrilled and wanted to compile a work to assist me if I had to do it again.

Therefore, this book is dedicated to the students at Lew Muckle Elementary School.

Arthur Petersen
Acknowledgments

When developing this project, I consulted many musicians, families, and friends to make this book a worthwhile and exciting venture. Therefore, thanks and appreciation are extended to my aunt Marion Petersen for always encouraging me and my cousin Atty. Diane Russell to move forward. I would be derelict to leave out my close, personal friend Annette Gereau who has always been there for me. She checks on me and is possibly the "Best Cook of all time." Andre Titus, Jr. is giving thanks for his listening ear and advising me along the way.

My sister Lisa is very special to me. Without her, I am sure that I would be lonely. My colleague at Lew Muckle Elementary, Yvonne Edwards Magloire, has been a supportive gem. Thanks!

I traveled to Danville, Virginia, the home of the opera singer Camilla Ella Williams and received additional information about her from people who knew her. My dear friend, Dr. Adele Allen's family, is from Danville, and she shared so many stories about Mrs. Williams.

Also, while in Danville, I had the opportunity to visit Peerman Brandon and his wife, Sharon. We sat, talked, and laughed; they fed me. I am thankful.

While in Havana, Cuba, in 2022, I discovered that music was everywhere, and I enjoyed it all. I asked about the classical singers as well as the contemporary ones. I got plenty of information and music, especially that of Pablo Milanés. I returned to Havana to bring in the New Year's

2023 and was greeted at the José Martí International Airport by Ojeda and Tamara Fortun. This time I enjoyed music and dinner with the family of Ojeda and Tamara Fortun. They thank and appreciate their kindness, openness, and love for music. Thank you to Dr. Nelson Hall, concert pianist, for introducing me to the Fortuns.

My friends in Ripoll O'Connor and Emmanuel Fields in Miami, Florida, have been there to pick me up from the Miami International Airport during the pandemic to use the Miami Edison Public Library in Liberty City and the Model City Public (among the few cultural centers opened during the pandemic).

The Librarians at the Edison Center Branch Library of the Miami-Dade Public Library System, Model City Branch Library of the Miami-Dade Public Library System, and e Saint John Vianney College Seminary Maytag Memorial Library are special. Without their assistance, this book will still be floating in my mind.

Arthur Petersen

Introduction

In stereotyping, when one thinks of classical music, one almost always thinks or believes it is reserved only for non-blacks. Well, that is just stereotypical. It is not new. Historically, Black people have always been connected to classical music and any art form involving rhythm, creativity, passion, performance, and analyzing the "why." **In classical music, it is interesting to note that** this world is blindingly white, both in its history and its present. The field must acknowledge a history of systemic racism while also honoring the individual experiences of Black composers, musicians, and listeners. Black people have long been marginalized, but they have never been outsiders.[1]

Joseph Bologne, Chevalier de Saint-Georges, born in 1745 in Guadeloupe to Nanon, an enslaved Senegalese mother, and Georges de Bologne Saint-Georges, Frenchman, had studied the violin in Paris, France, and had been conductor of the leading symphony orchestra in Paris.

Composer, conductor, and flutist Alton Augustus Adams, Sr, born in Charlotte Amalie, St. Thomas, Danish West Indies in 1889, became the first Black person to be a bandmaster for a Navy band.

In reading this work, you will see Blacks remain global and the ones in this book have devoted themselves to classical-

---
[1] Alex Ross, "Black Scholars Confront White Supremacy in Classical Music," https://www.newyorker.com/magazine/2020/09/21/black-scholars-confront-white-supremacy-in-classical-music.

music studies. This is not to insinuate that they have denied their culture and traditions. They all understand that the arts are political, and the struggle continues.

The author became interested in writing about this topic after hearing Howard University graduate Jessye Norman singing the seduction aria, *Mon cœur s'ouvre à ta voix*, from the second act of Camille Saint-Saëns' 1877 opera, *Samson and Delilah*. I was touched by the beauty of the composition, the agility in her voice, her interpretation, and how she could command the audience. I had never heard any song of any music genre so beautiful that I had to investigate further. Afterward, I rushed back to Lew Muckle Elementary School to share it with the music teacher.

When this writer considered titles for the book, the thought was who paved the way for these artists. Some would say it was Marian Anderson, a few might say Sissieretta Joyner, and even fewer would say Catalina Berroa Ojea. Regardless, a path has been cleared, and the divas are welcome to continue to add to history!

Part I: **SINGERS**

Joaquina Maria da Conceição Lapinha (1785-1812)

Image Ownership: Fair Usage

Soprano Joaquina Maria da Conceição Lapinha was born in 1785 to Maria da Lapa. She left Brazil in 1791 and performed in Portugal, thus becoming the first Black/Biracial singer to have performed in Portugal in 1795 at the Teatro Nacional de São Carlos. In 1805 Lapinha returned to her native land and maintained her profession as the *prima donna* of the Opera Nova in Rio de Janeiro. In 1811, she performed for John VI of Portugal in Rio de Janeiro.[2] Lapinha performed on Lusitanian and Carioca stages.[3]

---

[2] Rosana Marreco Orsini Brescia, "Half-Caste Actresses in Colonial Brazilian Opera Houses,"
https://www.mixedracestudies.org/?tag=joaquina-lapinha.
[3] "The singer Joaquina Lapinha: her contribution for the coloratura soprano repertoire in the Brazilian colonial period,"

I Paved the Way

Joaquina Maria da Conceição Lapinha died in 1812.

Sources:

Alexandra van Leeuwen, "The singer Joaquina Lapinha: her contribution for the coloratura soprano repertoire in the Brazilian colonial period," https://bv.fapesp.br/en/publicacao/76255/the-singer-joaquina-lapinha-her-contribution-for-the-colora/.

"Joaquina Lapinha – Harmonia," https://www.youtube.com/watch?v=R0B_gdshj4k.

Rosana Marreco Orsini Brescia, "Half-Caste Actresses in Colonial Brazilian Opera Houses," https://www.mixedracestudies.org/?tag=joaquina-lapinha.

---

https://bv.fapesp.br/en/publicacao/76255/the-singer-joaquina-lapinha-her-contribution-for-the-colora/.

Arthur Petersen
Elizabeth Greenfield Taylor (1809-1876)

Image Ownership: Public Domain

Elizabeth Greenfield (slave name) Taylor, the first African American opera singer, was born enslaved in 1809 in Natchez, Mississippi,[4] to Anna Greenfield and a man whose surname was Taylor. The first name has yet to be discovered. Elizabeth was given private singing lessons in Philadelphia, possibly by the Quakers.

---

[4] "Elizabeth Taylor Greenfield,"
https://www.nps.gov/people/elizabeth-taylor-greenfield.htm.

In 1851, Taylor was ordered to sing at the Buffalo Musical Association. However, she was later permitted to perform at the Home of Aged Colored Persons and the Colored Orphan Asylum.[5] In 1854, Taylor performed at Buckingham Palace in London. And two years later, in 1853, she made her classical voice debut at Metropolitan Hall in New York City, performing selected works of George Frideric Handel, Wolfgang Amadeus Mozart, Gioachino Rossini, Giacomo Meyerbeer, Vincenzo Bellini, and Gaetano Donizetti that attracted more than 4,000 music enthusiasts.

In the late 1860s, Taylor established and directed an opera ensemble in Philadelphia, Pennsylvania. Elizabeth Greenfield Taylor died in Philadelphia on March 31, 1876. She was 67.

Sources:

"Elizabeth Taylor Greenfield," https://www.nps.gov/people/elizabeth-taylor-greenfield.htm;

"Elizabeth Taylor Greenfield," https://www.thoughtco.com/elizabeth-taylor-greenfield-biography-45259.

---

[5] "Elizabeth Taylor Greenfield," https://www.thoughtco.com/elizabeth-taylor-greenfield-biography-45259.

Arthur Petersen
Matilda Sissieretta Joyner/Madame Jones (1869-1933)

Image Ownership: Public Domain

Matilda Sissieretta Joyner, Concert Singer, was born on January 5, 1869, in Portsmouth, Virginia to Jeremiah Joyner, a Baptist Minister and Henrietta Joyner, a singer and church musician.[6] In 1883, at the age of 14, Matilda

---

[6] " Matilda Sissieretta Joyner Jones,"
http://riheritagehalloffame.com/matilda-sissieretta-joyner-jones/.

married her manager David Richard Jones. It lasted one year.

There is no recorded evidence of Madame Jones performing in a concert hall or formal music studies.[7]

Madame Matilda Sissieretta Joyner Jones died on June 24, 1933, in Providence, Rhode Island. She was 64. In 1977, she was inducted into the Rhode Island Heritage Hall of Fame.[8]

Sources:

Ashawnta Jackson, "The Life of Matilda Sissieretta Jones," https://daily.jstor.org/the-life-of-matilda-sissieretta-jones.

Catherine Foster, "Sissieretta Joyner," https://www.blackpast.org/african-american-history/jones-sissieretta-1869-1933/;

" Matilda Sissieretta Joyner Jones," http://riheritagehalloffame.com/matilda-sissieretta-joyner-jones/.

---

[7] Ashawnta Jackson, "The Life of Matilda Sissieretta Jones," https://daily.jstor.org/the-life-of-matilda-sissieretta-jones.
[8] " Matilda Sissieretta Joyner Jones," http://riheritagehalloffame.com/matilda-sissieretta-joyner-jones/.

Arthur Petersen
Florence Cole-Talbert McCleave 1890-1961)

Image Ownership: Fair Usage

Florence Cole-Talbert McCleave, "Queen of the Concert Stage," was born on June 17, 1890, in Detroit, Michigan, to Thomas A. Cole, a bass singer and dramatic reader, and Sadie Chandler Cole, a mezzo-soprano and a former member of the Fisk Jubilee Singers. At an early age, Florence began voice and piano studies. However, she graduated from Los Angeles High School in California, thus being the first Black there. Afterward, she enrolled in the University of Southern California College of Music and traveled and performed with Hahn's Jubilee Singers.

Florence Cole married Wendall Talbert, a pianist/conductor, for a brief time. However, she chose to keep the name for professional reasons, as he was a known musician.

In 1916, Cole-Talbert moved to Chicago, Illinois, to further study at the Chicago Musical College, graduating in 1919. Also, a member of Delta Sigma Theta Sorority, Inc. and joint composer of the "Delta Hymn" with Alice Dunbar Nelson. In 1927, Cole-Talbert performed the title role in Giuseppe Verdi's *Aida* at the Teatro Communale in Cosenza, Italy. In 1930, she served as Director of Music at Bishop College (now Paul Quinn College) in Dallas, Texas, and as head of Fisk University's voice department in Nashville, Tennessee, and went on to head voice programs at Tuskegee Institute (University) and Alabama State College (University).

Florence Cole-Talbert McCleave, a co-founder of the Memphis Music Association, died on April 3, 1961, in Memphis, Tennessee. She was 71.

In 2017, Opera Memphis created and implemented The McCleave Project, an initiative to address the issues of equity and diversity in opera. And two years later, in 2019, Florence Cole-Talbert McCleave was inducted into the Memphis Music Hall of Fame.

Sources:

"Delta Sigma Theta Sorority, Inc.," https://m.facebook.com/dstinc1913/photos/a.187330364702445/945323502236457/?type=3.

"Florence Cole Talbert McCleave," https://memphismusichalloffame.com/inductee/florence-cole-talbert-mccleave/.

Florence Cole Talbert McCleave," https://www.flickr.com/photos/147039490@N04/27474777309;

The Memphis Hall of Fame, https://memphismusichalloffame.com/inductee/florence-cole-talbert-mccleave/.

Caterina Jarboro (1896-1986)

Image Ownership: Fair Usage

Caterina Jarboro, whose Christian name was Katherine Lee Yarborough, was born in 1896 in Wilmington, North Carolina, to a Black father and American Indian mother. She had two siblings, Joseph Jarboro and Anna Jarboro Gayle. [9] Caterina attended Gregory Normal School in Wilmington. However, after the death of her parents in 1916, Jarbora was taken to Brooklyn, New York, to her aunt's home.

Jarboro performed 1921 in Sissle and Blake's "Shuffle Along" in 1921. In 1930, she made her operatic debut in

---

[9] "Caterina Jarboro," https://www.nytimes.com/1986/08/16/obituaries/caterina-jarboro.html.

Giuseppe Verdi's Aida at the Puccini Theater in Milan, Italy. Three years later, in 1933, Alfredo she performed Aida with the Chicago Civic Opera at the New York Hippodrome Theater.[10] She was denied membership to the New Metropolitan Opera after they found out that she was not an Italian but a Black Indian. However, she performed a recital at Town Hall in 1942 and one in 1944 at Carnegie Hall.[11]

In 1955, Jarboro retired as a singer and was honored in 1975 at a ceremony in Wilmington, North Carolina's Thalian Hall, and in 1999, a star in her memory was placed on the city's Walk of Fame.[12] Caterina Jarboro died in Manhattan, New York in 1986. She was 90.[13]

Sources:

"An introduction to soprano Caterina Jarboro, the first female black singer to perform on a US opera stage," https://www.classical-music.com/features/artists/an-introduction-to-soprano-caterina-jarboro-the-first-female-black-singer-to-perform-on-a-us-opera-stage/.

---

[10] "An introduction to soprano Caterina Jarboro, the first female black singer to perform on a US opera stage," https://www.classical-music.com/features/artists/an-introduction-to-soprano-caterina-jarboro-the-first-female-black-singer-to-perform-on-a-us-opera-stage/.
[11] "Caterina Jarboro," https://www.nytimes.com/1986/08/16/obituaries/caterina-jarboro.html.
[12] "Caterina Jarboro," https://nhcpl.contentdm.oclc.org/digital/collection/p16072coll5/id/612/.
[13] "Caterina Jarboro," https://www.nytimes.com/1986/08/16/obituaries/caterina-jarboro.html.

"Caterina Jarboro," https://nhcpl.contentdm.oclc.org/digital/collection/p16072coll5/id/612/;

"Caterina Jarboro," https://www.nytimes.com/1986/08/16/obituaries/caterina-jarboro.html;

"Black Then: Discover Our History," https://blackthen.com/caterina-jarboro-first-female-black-opera-singer/.

Arthur Petersen

Marian Anderson (1897-1993)

Image Ownership: Fair Usage

Marian Anderson, a contralto, who led the way for numerous Black Classical singers, was born on February 27, 1897, in Philadelphia, Pennsylvania to John Berkley Anderson, a coal and ice dealer from King William County, Virginia, and Annie Delilah Rucker Anderson from Boonsboro, in Bedford County, Virginia.[14] Marian was the oldest daughter of three girls- Alyse (1900) and Ethel May (1902). Both sisters were singers, and they all sang at the Union Baptist Church when she was six years old. And at eight years old, she started formal piano studies. Her early education was at the Stanton Grammar School with only

---

[14] Allan Keiler, "Marian Anderson: A Singer's Journey," https://archive.nytimes.com/www.nytimes.com/books/first/k/keiler-anderson.html.

white teachers as the policy did not include black teachers in all-white or mixed schools.[15]

After the death of Marian's father in 1912, the family experienced financial constraints that created disruption with her high school education. However, she continued singing while assisting with the noble obligations of assisting financially at home.[16]

Image Ownership: Fair Usage

In 1927, Anderson travelled to Europe because she saw that it was a place of absolute freedom and culture where she could perfect her musical skills. However, most of her time there was spent in Germany studying and performing German Lieder and she went on to Scandinavia for more performance.[17]

---

[15] Ibid.
[16] Allan Keiler, "Marian Anderson: A Singer's Journey," https://archive.nytimes.com/www.nytimes.com/books/first/k/keiler-anderson.html.
[17] "Marian Anderson," https://www.imdb.com/name/nm0993450/bio.

In 1934, in Paris, Anderson was offered a guaranteed of 15 concerts with a fee of $500 per concert by the Russian impresario Solomon Izrailevich Gurkov, who managed many performing artists. Through Gurkov, Anderson became the third-highest box office in the area and was also invited to the Moscow Art.[18]

In 1939, Anderson was denied a performance at The Daughters of the American Revolution's (DAR) Constitution Hall because of the color of her skin. Because of the treatment of Anderson, First Lady Eleanor Roosevelt, who had been a member of DAR resigned.[19]

In 1986, United States President Ronald Reagan presented Anderson with the National Medal of Arts.[20] Marian Anderson died on April 8, 1993, in Portland, Oregon. She was 96

Sources:

Allan Keiler, "Marian Anderson: A Singer's Journey," https://archive.nytimes.com/www.nytimes.com/books/first/k/keiler-anderson.html;

"Marian Anderson,' http://marian-anderson.com/biography/;

"Marian Anderson," https://www.imdb.com/name/nm0993450/bio;

---

[18] "Marian Anderson," https://www.imdb.com/name/nm0993450/bio.
[19] "Marian Anderson biography and timeline," https://www.pbs.org/wnet/americanmasters/marian-anderson-biography-and-timeline/20235.
[20] "Marian Anderson,' http://marian-anderson.com/biography/.

"Marian Anderson biography and timeline," https://www.pbs.org/wnet/americanmasters/marian-anderson-biography-and-timeline/20235.

Arthur Petersen

Aisha Musa Ahmad (1905-1974)

Image Ownership: Fair Usage

Aisha Musa Ahmad, a Sudanese singer, was born in Kassala, Sudan, in 1905 to Musa Ahmad Yahiyya, a Fulani religious scholar, and Hujra, a Hausa. The first child of seven, Ahmad was educated in her father's school-Khalwa in Omdurman, Sudan. Aisha was also known as Aisha al-Falatiya.

Singing professionally at 14, Ahmad started out reciting her lessons from the Quran, the central religious text of Islam. However, Ahmad moved on to tom-tom songs and Sudanese Art Songs by Sudanese poets. She often performed in Sudanese coffeehouses, and in 1942, she became the first woman to sing on Sudanese radio and recorded more than 150 songs.

Aisha Musa Ahmad, married twice to Ibrahim Adbarawi and Jiddu Kabli, died in Omdurman, Sudan, on February 24, 1974. She was 69.

Sources:

"Aisha Musa Ahmad," https://21dialogues21.org/aisha-musa-ahmad/.

"Aisha Musa Ahmad," https://worddisk.com/Aisha_Musa_Ahmad/;

"Aisha Musa Ahmad (1905-1974)," https://www.ufrgs.br/africanas/aisha-musa-ahmad-1905-1974/.

Dorothy Leigh Maynor (1910-1996)

Image Ownership: Fair Usage

Dorothy Leigh Mainor was born in Norfolk, Virginia on September 3, 1910, to John J. Mainor, a Methodist minister and Alice Jefferson Mainor.

Dorothy graduated from Hampton Institute, now Hampton University in 1933 and was a prodigy of the renowned African Canadian composer and pianist R. Nathaniel Dett. He composed six settings of Negro spirituals, especially for her.[21]

In 1935, Maynor earned a Bachelor of Music degree in Choral Conducting from Westminster Choir College in Princeton, New Jersey[22] now located in Lawrenceville, New Jersey at Rider University.

---

[21] "Dorothy Maynor Biography," https://afrovoices.com/dorothy-maynor-biography/.
[22] "Dorothy Maynor Biography," https://afrovoices.com/dorothy-maynor-biography/.

I Paved the Way

In 1939, Maynor debuted with the Boston Symphony Orchestra at Town Hall in New York City and the following year in 1940, she was awarded a Town Hall Endowment Series Award for the earlier performance.

Maynor was the first African American to sing at a presidential inauguration. In 1949, she performed at United States President Harry S. Truman 's inaugural gala and in 1953 at U.S. President Dwight D. Eisenhower's 1953 presidential inauguration at Constitution Hall.[23]

In 1964, Maynor founded the Harlem School of the Arts which began with 20 students and by 1979, there were 1,000.

Maynard was awarded honorary doctorates from Howard University, Oberlin Conservatory of Music, Hartt School of Music, and Westminster Choir College. In 1975, she became.

Dorothy Maynor, the first African American on the board of directors of the Metropolitan Opera, died on February 19, 1996, in West Chester, Pennsylvania. She was 85.

Sources:

"Dorothy Maynor Biography,"
https://afrovoices.com/dorothy-maynor-biography/.

"Harlem's Dorothy Maynor Harlem School Of The Arts Founder And A Woman Of Many Firsts,"
https://www.harlemworldmagazine.com/harlems-dorothy-

---

[23] "Harlem's Dorothy Maynor Harlem School Of The Arts Founder And A Woman Of Many Firsts,"
https://www.harlemworldmagazine.com/harlems-dorothy-maynor-harlem-school-of-the-arts-founder-and-a-woman-of-many-firsts/.

maynor-harlem-school-of-the-arts-founder-and-a-woman-of-many-firsts/.

I Paved the Way
Camilla Ella Williams (1919-2012)

Image Ownership: Fair Usage

On October 18, 1919, Camilla Ella Williams was born in Danville, Virginia, to Cornelius Booker Williams, a chauffeur, and Fannie Carey Williams. Camilla's siblings were Cornelius Booker Williams, Jr., Mary Williams, and Helen Williams.[24]

Williams began piano lessons when she was eight years old with the choir director at Calvary Baptist Church in Danville. She attended the public school system and graduated from John M. Langston High School, graduating as class valedictorian in 1937. Afterward, she went on to receive a Bachelor of Science degree in Music Education at Virginia State College for Negroes, now Virginia State University in 1941. That same year, Williams returned to Danville and accepted a position as a teacher.[25]

---

[24] Margalit Fox, "Camilla Williams, Barrier-Breaking Opera Star, Dies at 92," https://www.nytimes.com/2012/02/03/arts/music/camilla-williams-opera-singer-dies-at-92.html.
[25] "Camilla Williams," https://www.danvillemuseum.org/content/uploads/PDF/exhibits/camilla/camilla_book_cover.pdf.

In 1943, Williams competed in voice in Philadelphia and won a Marian Anderson Award. The following year in 1944, she received the competitive award again.

Two years later, in 1946, Williams made her debut with the New York City Opera performing the title role in Giacomo Puccini's *Madama Butterfly*.[26] Eight years later in 1954, Williams made history when she performed the title role in *Madama Butterfly* with the Vienna State Opera in Austria, she was the first Black to do so.[27]

In 1977, Williams joined the voice faculty at Jacobs School of Music of Indiana University Williams, thus becoming the first African American Professor of Voice there. appointed to in 1977. Seven years later in 1984, the Central Conservatory of Music in Beijing, China hired Williams to teach voice performance pedagogy; making her the first African American there as well.

---

[26] Margalit Fox, "Camilla Williams, Barrier-Breaking Opera Star, Dies at 92," https://www.nytimes.com/2012/02/03/arts/music/camilla-williams-opera-singer-dies-at-92.html.

[27] "Camilla Ella Williams, (1919-2012), https://edu.lva.virginia.gov/changemakers/items/show/269.

I Paved the Way

Image Ownership: Fair Usage

Williams was not only an artist and educator; she was politically conscience. During the 1960s when there was turbulence throughout the country regarding civil rights for African Americans, she sang "The Star-Spangled Banner" at the White House and sang the anthem before more than 250,000 people at the Lincoln Memorial, before Martin Luther King Jr. delivered his "I Have a Dream" speech.

Camilla Ella Williams died on January 29, 2012, in Bloomington, Indiana. She was 92.

Sources:

"Camilla Williams," https://www.danvillemuseum.org/content/uploads/PDF/exhibits/camilla/camilla_book_cover.pdf.

"Camilla Ella Williams, (1919-2012), https://edu.lva.virginia.gov/changemakers/items/show/269.

Margalit Fox, "Camilla Williams, Barrier-Breaking Opera Star, Dies at 92," https://www.nytimes.com/2012/02/03/arts/music/camilla-williams-opera-singer-dies-at-92.html.

I Paved the Way
Charlotte Wesley Holloman (1922-2015)

Image Ownership: Fair Usage

Charlotte Wesley Holloman was born in Washington, D.C. in the predominately Black community of Georgetown to Charles Harris Wesley, a historian and president of Central State University, and Florence Louise Johnson Wesley, an English Teacher on March 24, 1922. mother was an English teacher Charlotte attended the DC Public Schools, graduating in 1937 from the prestigious all-Black graduated from Dunbar High School. Afterward, she enrolled in Howard University School of Music, receiving a Bachelor of Music degree in Voice and Piano in 1941. In 1943, she earned a Master of Arts degree in Voice and Music Education from Columbia University in New York.[28]

In 1944, Charlotte married John L. S. Holloman Jr., a medical doctor and they parented a daughter, Charlotte.

In 1952, Holloman appeared in *My Darlin' Aida*, a version of Giuseppe Verdi's opera *Aida*.[29] In addition, she performed with several opera companies with opera companies in Ruhr and Saarbrücken, Germany performing in Giacomo Puccini's *Madama Butterfly* and *Tosca* as well as in Wolfgang Amadeus Mozart's *The Magic Flute*.[30]

Returning to the United States, Holloman taught voice at Howard University, the University of the District of Columbia, and the Catholic University of America, and accompanied musicians throughout the DC area.[31]

Charlotte Wesley Holloman, a member of Delta Sigma Theta Sorority, Inc., died on July 30, 2015. She was 93.

Sources:

Adam Bernstein, "Charlotte Holloman, concert singer and voice teacher, dies at 93," https://www.washingtonpost.com/people/adam-bernstein/.

---

[28] Erika Weber, "Charlotte Wesley Holloman," https://www.blackpast.org/african-american-history/holloman-charlotte-wesley-1922-2015/.
[29] Adam Bernstein, "Charlotte Holloman, concert singer and voice teacher, dies at 93," https://www.washingtonpost.com/people/adam-bernstein/.
[30] Fred Plotkin, "Discovering Charlotte Wesley Holloman," https://www.wqxr.org/story/discovering-charlotte-wesley-holloman/.
[31] Fred Plotkin, "Discovering Charlotte Wesley Holloman," https://www.wqxr.org/story/discovering-charlotte-wesley-holloman.

Erika Weber, "Charlotte Wesley Holloman," https://www.blackpast.org/african-american-history/holloman-charlotte-wesley-1922-2015/;

Fred Plotkin, "Discovering Charlotte Wesley Holloman," https://www.wqxr.org/story/discovering-charlotte-wesley-holloman/.

Arthur Petersen

Muriel Burrell Smith (1923-1985)

Image Ownership: Fair Usage

Mezzo-Soprano Muriel Burrell Smith was born on February 23, 1923, in Harlem, New York City, to Sigourney Burrell Smith and Olive Gilmore Smith.[32]

In 1939, Smith began her formal music studies at the Curtis Institute of Music in Philadelphia, Pennsylvania. She was the first African American to attend the prestigious institution. She graduated in 1946.

In 1943, Smith made her début on Broadway as Carmen Jones in a version of Georges Bizet's Carmen.

---

[32] "Muriel Burrell Smith," https://www.encyclopedia.com/women/dictionaries-thesauruses-pictures-and-press-releases/smith-muriel-burrell-1923-1985.

In 1949 she starred in South Pacific and The King and I in London, England. And in 1956, she performed Carmen again, but this time Smith was at the Royal Opera House in London.[33] And four years later, in 1960, she made the film The Crowning Experience, portraying the life of the African American educator Mary McLeod Bethune.

In the 1970s, while caring for her aging mother in Richmond, Virginia, Smith accepted a position at Virginia Union University teaching voice performance pedagogy. Muriel Burrell Smith died in Richmond, Virginia, on September 13, 1985.[34] She was 62.

Sources:

"Mezzo-Soprano Muriel Burrell Smith (1923-1985)," https://wap.org.ng/read/mezzo-soprano-muriel-burrell-smith-1923-1985/.

"Muriel Burrell Smith," https://www.encyclopedia.com/women/dictionaries-thesauruses-pictures-and-press-releases/smith-muriel-burrell-1923-1985;

"Muriel Burrell Smith Dies," https://www.washingtonpost.com/archive/local/1985/09/16/muriel-burrell-smith-dies/a6ce61f9-ac81-494c-8d67-84f188bb9a3e/.

---

[33] "Mezzo-Soprano Muriel Burrell Smith (1923-1985)," https://wap.org.ng/read/mezzo-soprano-muriel-burrell-smith-1923-1985/.
[34] "Muriel Burrell Smith Dies," https://www.washingtonpost.com/archive/local/1985/09/16/muriel-burrell-smith-dies/a6ce61f9-ac81-494c-8d67-84f188bb9a3e/.

Arthur Petersen
Mattiwilda Dobbs (1925-2015)

Image Ownership: Fair Usage

Mattiwilda Dobbs was born July 11, 1925, in Atlanta, Georgia to John Wesley Dobbs and the former Irene Ophelia Thompson Dobbs.[35] She received the Bachelor of Arts degree in music from Spelman College in Atlanta, Georgia, in 1946. To be sure, she was the class valedictorian. Four years later, in 1950, she earned a Master of arts degree in Spanish from Columbia University in New

---

[35]Margalit Fox, "Mattiwilda Dobbs, Soprano and Principal at Met, Dies at 90,"
https://www.nytimes.com/2015/12/11/arts/music/mattiwilda-dobbs-black-soprano-and-principal-at-met-dies-at-90.html.

York. Afterward, she immediately traveled to Paris on a two-year fellowship to study with Pierre Viernac.[36]

In 1951 she won first prize at the Geneva Competition in Switzerland. From 1952 to 1954, Dobbs appeared in opera in Europe and performed in Stravinsky's Nightingale at the Holland Festival in Amsterdam, the Queen of the Night in Mozart's *The Magic Flute* at Genoa, Zerbinetta in Strauss' *Ariadne auf Naxos* at the Glyndebounce Opera Festival, Gilda in Rigoletto, and Olympia in The Tales of Hoffman at the Royal Opera House in London.

Dobbs was the first Black opera star to sing at La Scala in Milan, Italy, and the first Black soprano to sing at the New York Metropolitan Opera.[37]

In the 1970s, Dobbs taught music at Spelman College and Howard University.
Mattiwilda Dobbs died in Atlanta, Georgia, on December 8, 2015. She was 90.

Sources:

Karla Rixon, "Mattiwilda Dobbs," https://www.blackpast.org/african-american-history/dobbs-mattiwilda-1925/.

Margalit Fox, "Mattiwilda Dobbs, Soprano and Principal at Met, Dies at 90," https://www.nytimes.com/2015/12/11/arts/music/mattiwild

---

[36] Karla Rixon, "Mattiwilda Dobbs," https://www.blackpast.org/african-american-history/dobbs-mattiwilda-1925/

[37] "Mattiwilda Dobbs," https://samepassage.org/mattiwilda-dobbs/.

a-dobbs-black-soprano-and-principal-at-met-dies-at-90.html.

"Mattiwilda Dobbs," https://samepassage.org/mattiwilda-dobbs/.

Adele Addison Berger (1925-)

Image Ownership: Fair Usage

Adele Addison Berger was born in Harlem, New York, on July 24, 1925. She received a scholarship to study music at the Westminster Choir College in Princeton, New Jersey, and earned a Bachelor of Music degree in Voice in 1946. In 1948, Berger obtained a Master of Arts degree from Princeton University.[38]

---

[38] "Adele Addison, Opera Vocalist, born," https://aaregistry.org/story/adelle-addison-one-of-o.

In 1952, Berger made her classical debut as a recitalist at New York's Town Hall. And three years later, in 1955, she debuted with the New York City Opera as Mimi in Giacomo Puccini's opera in four acts, *La Bohème*.

Berger performed solo work in 1956 with the Howard University Chorale under the direction of Warner Lawson and the National Symphony Orchestra.

In 1958, Adele married Norman Berger in Springfield, Massachusetts,[39] and the following year, 1959, she premiered with the Boston Symphony Orchestra singing in Francis Poulenc's Gloria.

Berger has received numerous accolades throughout her career, including honorary doctorates from the University of Massachusetts and the Manhattan School of Music.[40]

Sources:

"Adele Addison," https://wbssmedia.com/artists/detail/1667.

"Adele Addison, Opera Vocalist, born," https://aaregistry.org/story/adelle-addison-one-of-o;

Otis Alexander, "Adele Addison Berger," https://www.blackpast.org/african-american-history/people-african-american-history/adele-addison-berger-1925/.

---

[39] "Adele Addison," https://wbssmedia.com/artists/detail/1667.
[40] Otis Alexander, "Adele Addison Berger," https://www.blackpast.org/african-american-history/people-african-american-history/adele-addison-berger-1925/.

I Paved the Way
Mary Leontyne Price (1927-)

Image Ownership: Fair Usage
Photography by Jack Mitchell

Born on February 10, 1927, in Laurel, Mississippi to James Anthony, a carpenter and Katherine Baker Price, a midwife, Mary Violet Leontyne Price, was the first African American soprano showcased at an international level. She had one brother George Price.

Price made her operatic debut in 1961 in the New York Metropolitan Opera production of Giuseppe Verdi's *Il Trovatore* as Leonora[41] and has since performed leading roles in major operas globally. However, she is known for her creative contribution as Aida in Verdi's *Aida*.

Price, Who was married to an opera singer, William Warfield, received the Bachelor of Arts degree from Central State University in Wilberforce, Ohio.

Price is the recipient of a plethora of awards and accolades, in including receiving the Grammy Lifetime Achievement Award in 1988, Primetime Emmy Award for Outstanding Individual Achievement in Classical Music or Dance Programming in 1984, Grammy Award for Best Classical Vocal Solo in 1960, 1963, 1964, 1965, 1966, 1967, 1968, 1971, 1973, 1974, 1980 and 1982. [42]

Sources:

"Leontyne Price," http://awardsandwinners.com/winner/?mid=/m/025027.

"Leontyne Price, Legendary Diva, Is a Movie Star at 90," https://www.nytimes.com/2017/12/22/arts/music/leontyne-price-met-opera.html.

---

[41] "Leontyne Price, Legendary Diva, Is a Movie Star at 90," https://www.nytimes.com/2017/12/22/arts/music/leontyne-price-met-opera.html.
[42] "Leontyne Price," http://awardsandwinners.com/winner/?mid=/m/025027.

Gloria Davy (1931-2012)

Spinto soprano Gloria Davy, with roots from the Caribbean island of Saint Vincent, was born on March 29, 1931, in Brooklyn, New York, and graduated from P.S. 129 in Brooklyn, the High School of Music and Art in 1951. She was trained at the Juilliard School, receiving the Bachelor of Arts degree in voice performance in 1953. She performed the title role in Giuseppe Verdi's *Aida* in Nice, Bologna. In 1957, Davy premiered in Hans Wernber Henze's Nachtstücke und Arien, and in 1959 she married Herman Penningsfield, a Swiss stockbroker. They parented a son, Jean-Marc Penningsfeld. From 1961–1968 Davy was a resident artist at the Berlin State Opera in Germany. And from 1984-1997, Davy taught voice at Indiana University in Bloomington, Indiana.

Gloria Davy died on November 28, 2012, in Geneva, Switzerland. She was 81.

Sources:

"Gloria Davy," https://www.ibdb.com/broadway-cast-staff/gloria-davy-107458.

"Gloria Davy," https://m.imdb.com/name/nm2240221/;

"Gloria Davy, February 22, 1958," https://radar.auctr.edu/islandora/object/auc.034%3A0120_008.

"Gloria Davy, the First African American to sing Aida at the Met, has Died," https://www.operanews.com/Opera_News_Magazine/2012/12/News/Gloria_Davy.html.

Margalit Fox, "Gloria Davy, First African American to Sing Aida at the Met, Dies at 81," https://www.nytimes.com/2012/12/11/arts/music/gloria-davy-first-african-american-to-sing-aida-at-the-met-dies-at-81.html.

Shirley Verrett (1931-2010)

Image Ownership: Fair Usage

Shirley Verrett was born in New Orleans, Louisiana, on May 31, 1931.[43] However, she was reared in Los Angeles,

---

[43] "Shirley Verrett Obituary," https://www.theguardian.com/music/2010/nov/08/shirley-verrett-obituary.

California. In 1961 she won the Metropolitan Opera National Council Auditions.

In 1957, Verrett made her operatic debut in Britten's *The Rape of Lucretia*, and in 1958, she debuted as Irina in Kurt Weill's *Lost in the Stars* with the New York City Opera. A year later, in 1959, she performed in Nicolas Nabokov's *Rasputins Tod* in Cologne, Germany.

Verrett made her debut at the Metropolitan Opera in 1968 with *Carmen an*d at La Scala in 1969 in *Samson and Dalila.*[44]

In 1996 Verrett became faculty of Voice of the University of Michigan School of Music, Theatre & Dance in Ann Arbor, Michigan.

Shirley Verrett died on November 5, 2010, in Ann Arbor, Michigan,.[45] She was 79.

Sources:

"Shirley Verrett Obituary," https://www.theguardian.com/music/2010/nov/08/shirley-verrett-obituary.

---

[44] "Shirley Verrett Obituary," https://www.theguardian.com/music/2010/nov/08/shirley-verrett-obituary.
[45] "Shirley Verrett," https://www.imdb.com/name/nm0894854/bio.

Ella Ruth Lee (1933-2013)

Image Ownership: Fair Usage

Ella Ruth Lee was born on June 10, 1933, to Winston Lee and Mary Ella Lee in Tyler, Texas. She was reared in Los Angeles and began piano lessons there. From 1947 to 1951, Lee was a student and member of the choir at Jefferson High School in South Los Angeles. After graduating in 1952, she enrolled in Los Angeles State College of Applied Arts and

Sciences where she received a Bachelor of Arts degree in music in 1955.[46]

Lee performed principal roles throughout Europe and the United States for more than thirty years, made her operatic debut in 1960, performing the role of the Ethiopian Princess in Giuseppe Verdi's *Aida* in the Guild Opera Company in Los Angeles. In 1963, Lee performed the soprano role of "Floria Tosca" in Giacomo Puccini's *Tosca* with the Komische Oper Berlin in East Berlin, Germany. [47]

During Lee's artistic career, she performed *Aida* more than 500 times with numerous opera companies, throughout Austria, Germany, the United Kingdom, the and United States.

Ella Ruth Lee retired from the opera stage in 2000. She died on September 16, 2013, in Los Angeles, California. She was 80.

Sources:

"All About Ella Ruth Lee Biography: Career, Family, Songs, and Death," https://howafrica.com/all-about-ella-ruth-lee-biography-career-family-songs-and-death/.

"Ella Ruth Lee Romani (1933-2013),"blacknewszone.com › ella-ruth-lee-romani-1933-2013.

---

[46] "All About Ella Ruth Lee Biography: Career, Family, Songs, and Death," https://howafrica.com/all-about-ella-ruth-lee-biography-career-family-songs-and-death/.
[47] "Ella Ruth Lee Romani (1933-2013)," blacknewszone.com › ella-ruth-lee-romani-1933-2013.

Martina Arroyo (1937-)

Image Ownership: Fair Usage

Spinto Soprano Martina Arroyo, who lives in Saint Croix, Virgin Islands, was born on February 2, 1937, to Demetrio Arroyo, from Puerto Rico and a mechanical engineer at the

Brooklyn Navy Yard, and Lucille Washington, a classical pianist from Charleston, South Carolina.

After graduating from Hunter College High School in in New York in 1953; at 16, Arroyo attended Hunter College, where she earned a Bachelor of Arts degree in Spanish at 19 from Hunter College in New York in 1956. And by the age of 20, in 1957, she completed a Master of Arts degree in comparative literature at New York University. Her thesis was "Ignacio Silone's Pane e Vino and Vino e Pane."

Arroyo made her American debut in Ildebrando Pizzetti's *Assassinio nella cattedrale* at Carnegie Hall in 1958

From 1965 to 1978, Arroyo was one of the lead women of the New York Metropolitan Opera. In addition, she has performed extensively internationally at stages La Scala in Italy, the Opéra National de Paris, the Vienna State Opera, and the Lyric Opera of Chicago. And in 1981, Arroyo received an honorary Doctor of Humane Letters from Hunter College.

In 1987, Arroyo performed the title role in Turandot with the Seattle Opera in Seattle, Washington. Two years later, in 1989, Martina Arroyo retired from opera performance. However, she continued to lecture at many institutions of higher learning, including Indiana University, Wilberforce University in Wilberforce, Ohio, and International Sommerakademie-Mozarteum in Salzburg, Austria.

In 2010, Martina Arroyo received the Opera Honors Award from the National Endowment for the Arts. She had 199 performances at the New York Metropolitan Opera.

Sources:

Anne Midgette, "From rising star to the grande dame, Martina Arroyo never forgot who she was," https://www.washingtonpost.com/entertainment/music/from-rising-star-to-grande-dame-martina-arroyo-never-forgot-who-she-was/2013/12/05/39958edc-5798-11e3-835d-e7173847c7cc_story.html.

"Hunter Congratulates Opera Singer Martina Arroyo '56, Recipient of the 2013 Kennedy Center Honors," https://www.hunter.cuny.edu/communications/pressroom/news/hunter-congratulates-opera-singer-martina-arroyo-201956-2013-recipient-of-the-kennedy-center-honors.

"Martina Arroya," https://www.kennedy-center.org/artists/a/ao-az/martina-arroyo/;

"Spinto Soprano Martina Arroyo," https://www.martinaarroyo.com/.

Arthur Petersen

Grace Melzia Bumbry (1937-2010)

Image Ownership: Fair Usage

Mezzo-Soprano Grace Melzia Bumbry was born in St. Louis, Missouri on January 4, 1937 to Benjamin James Bumbry a freight handler for a railroad company and Melzia Bumbry, a schoolteacher. Grace had two brothers, Benjamin James Bumbry, Jr. and Charles Bumbry. They were all singers. Grace's first music lessons came from her mother who taught her piano.[48]

---

[48] "Grace Bumbry," https://musicianguide.com/biographies/1608000604/Grace-Bumbry.htm.

Grace attended the prestigious segregated Sumner High School and during her senior year in 1954, St. Louis radio station KMOX held a teenage talent contest and Grace entered. She won a $1,000 war bond, a $1,000 scholarship to the St. Louis Institute of Music, and a free trip to New York City. After leaving high school, Bumbry studied at Boston University College of Fine Arts in Massachusetts. However, she transferred to Northwestern University in Evanston, Illinois. She went on to further study voice at the Music Academy of the West in Santa Barbara, California.[49]

Bumbry was not interested in performing opera but was fascinated with the world of German lieder and French mélodies. However, in 1958, Bumbry was one of the winners of the Metropolitan Opera National Council Auditions and went on to debut with l'Opéra de Paris in 1960 performing Amneris in Giuseppe Verdi's Aida. She was the first African American or person of color to perform at the opera hall.[50]

In 1961, Bumbry performed the role of Venus in Richard Wagner's Tannhäuser at the Bayreuth Festival in Bavaria, Germany. Bumbry's performance was so stunning with a gorgeous voice and memorable acting skills that the audience applauded for 30 minutes, with 42 curtain calls. In 1964, Bumbry debuted at the Vienna State Opera in Austria in Verdi's Lady Macbeth.

In 2009, President Barack Obama, presented to Bumbry the most prestigious and coveted award in America for one's contribution to the arts, The Kennedy Center Honors. The next year in 2010, she In portrayed"Monisha" in Scott

---

[49] "Grace Bumbry,"https://musicianguide.com/biographies/1608000604/Grace-Bumbry.htm.
[50] "Grace Bumbry,"https://gracebumbry.com/biography/.

Joplin's "Treemonisha" at the Theatre du Chatelet in Paris, France.[51]

Grace Bumbry holds honorary doctorates from St. Louis University, Rockhurst College, Kansas City, and University of Missouri.

Sources:

"Grace Bumbry," https://musicianguide.com/biographies/1608000604/Grace-Bumbry.html;

"Grace Bumbry,"https://gracebumbry.com/biography/;

Part of the Singers on Singing: Signature Roles series, " Singers on Singing: Grace Bumbry discusses Amneris," https://hampsongfoundation.org/resource/singers-on-singing-grace-bumbry-discusses-amneris/.

---

[51] "Grace Bumbry,"https://gracebumbry.com/biography/.

Jessye Norman (1945-2019)

Image Ownership: Fair Usage

Jessye Norman was born on September 15, 1945, in Augusta, Georgia to Silas Norman, an insurance broker and Janie Norman, a public schoolteacher.

At 17 years old, she earned a full-tuition scholarship to Howard University School of Music in Washington, DC, for Voice Performance,[52] where she studied with Carolyn Grant and sang in the University Choir under the directorship of the renowned Warren Lawson. In 1967, Norman received a Bachelor of Music degree.[53] Two years later in 1969, in Berlin, Germany, Norman made her debut on the operatic stage performing the role of Elisabeth in Richard Wagner's *Tannhäuser*.[54]

In 1972, Norman debuted in Giuseppe Verdi's Aida at Italy's most famous cultural center, Teatro alla Scala. She made her debut with the New York Metropolitan Opera in 1983, singing the role of "Cassandre" in Hector Berlioz's *Les Troyens*. In 1998, Norman was awarded a Doctor of Music for her services to music from the University of Pennsylvania in Philadelphia, Pennsylvania.[55]

Norman won her first Grammy at the 27th Annual Grammy Awards in 1985, at Shrine Auditorium, Los Angeles, for *Ravel: Songs Of Maurice Ravel* **in the Best Classical Vocal Soloist Performance category.**[56]

---

[52] Amir Vera and Pierre Meilhan, "Jessye Norman, international opera star, dead at 74," https://www.cnn.com/2019/09/30/entertainment/jessye-norman-obit/index.html.
[53] "Jessye Norman," https://thedig.howard.edu/featured-people/jessye-norman.
[54] Linnea Crowther, "Jessye Norman (1945–2019), Grammy-winning opera singer," https://www.legacy.com/news/celebrity-deaths/jessye-norman-1945-2019-grammy-winning-opera-singer/.
[55] "University of Pennsylvania, Honorary Degree Recipients," https://secretary.upenn.edu/ceremonies/honorary-degree-recipients/alphabetical/n.
[56] Amir Vera and Pierre Meilhan, "Jessye Norman, international opera star, dead at 74," https://www.cnn.com/2019/09/30/entertainment/jessye-norman-obit/index.html.

In 2003, the Jessye Norman School of the Arts opened in Augusta, Georgia, to provide free education in the arts to underrepresented children.[57] And in 2009, she was honored with the National Medal of Arts.[58]

Jessye Norman died on September 30, 2019, in New York City. She was 74.

Sources:

Amir Vera and Pierre Meilhan, "Jessye Norman, international opera star, dead at 74," https://www.cnn.com/2019/09/30/entertainment/jessye-norman-obit/index.html;

"Jessye Norman," https://thedig.howard.edu/featured-people/jessye-norman;

Linnea Crowther, "Jessye Norman (1945–2019), Grammy-winning opera singer," https://www.legacy.com/news/celebrity-deaths/jessye-norman-1945-2019-grammy-winning-opera-singer/.

"University of Pennsylvania, Honorary Degree Recipients," https://secretary.upenn.edu/ceremonies/honorary-degree-recipients/alphabetical/n.

---

[57] Ibid.
[58] Linnea Crowther, "Jessye Norman (1945–2019), Grammy-winning opera singer," https://www.legacy.com/news/celebrity-deaths/jessye-norman-1945-2019-grammy-winning-opera-singer/.

Arthur Petersen
Kathleen Deanna Battle (1948-)

Image Ownership: Fair Usage

Kathleen Deanna Battle was born on August 13, 1948 in Portsmouth, Ohio. She graduated from Portsmouth High School in 1966. Afterward, she was awarded a full scholarship to the University of Cincinnati – College-Conservatory of Music, where she received a Bachelor of Music Education degree in voice in 1970 and earned a Master of Education degree in Music Education in 1971. Battle made her opera debut in 1975 as Rosina in Gioachino Rossini's The Barber of Seville with Detroit's Michigan Opera Theatre in Detroit. And in 1976, she was singing Susanna in Mozart's The Marriage of Figaro with the New York City Opera.

However, Battle's most impressive works appealing to the masses were the collaboration with the world-renowned trumpeter Wynton Marsalis in a recording of baroque arias, Baroque Duet in 1993 and the 1998 collaboration with jazz pianist Herbie Hancock on his album Gershwin's World in an arrangement of Gershwin's Prelude in C♯ minor.

Battle's intellectual ability, talent, resilience has gotten her many Grammy Awards, including Best Opera Recording For "R. Strauss: Ariadne Auf Naxos" and Best Classical Vocal Soloist Performance for "Salzburg Recital" in 1988, Best Classical Vocal Performance for "Kathleen Battle At Carnegie Hall in 1993, Best Opera Recording of "Handel: Semele" in 1994.[59]

In addition, Battle is the recipient of honorary doctorates from Amherst College, Ohio University, Seton Hall University, University of Cincinnati, Westminster Choir College, and Xavier University. In 1999, Battle was inducted into the NAACP Image Hall of Fame.[60]

Kathleen Deanne Battle has performed internationally at many opera houses, including the English National Opera, Grand Théâtre de Genève, Vienna State Opera, and Deutsche Oper Berlin.

Sources:

"Kathleen Battle's Awards, "https://m.imdb.com/name/nm0061513/awards;

"Kathleen Battle, "https://www.u-s-history.com/pages/h3854.html

---

[59] "Kathleen Battle's Awards, "https://m.imdb.com/name/nm0061513/awards.
[60] "Kathleen Battle," https://www.u-s-history.com/pages/h3854.html.

Lorraine Elizabeth Baa (1953-2021)

Image Ownership: Fair Usage

Lorraine Elizabeth Baa (Gidron) was born in Charlotte Amalie, Virgin Islands, on February 1, 1953, to Orlando J. Baa, Sr.[61] and Rosalia Potter Baa. She had three siblings, Enid Maria Baa, Orlando J. Baa, Jr., and Louise Baa.

Baa graduated with honors from Saints Peter and Paul Catholic School in Charlotte Amalie in 1971, was a member of the school's Concert Mixed Chorus and studied and performed opera and Ballet on the island of St. Thomas. She

---

[61] "Orlando Baa," https://www.myheritage.com/names/orlando_baa.

was a member of the Fisk Jubilee Singers at Fisk University in Nashville, Tennessee where she received a Bachelor of Arts degree in Museology/Museum Studies in 1975.

In 1976, Baa was crowned Miss U.S. Virgin Islands and went on to compete at the Miss Universe pageant.

In 2010, Baa earned a Master of Arts in Biblical Studies from Friends International Christian University in Merced, California. A year later in 2011, she became the 33rd President of the Rotary Club of St. Thomas II and the seventh woman to lead the local branch of this international organization.

In 2016, Baa was President of Baa & Company LLC, a consulting firm.

A Delta Sigma Theta sorority, Sorority member and mother of Ricky Gidron, III,[62] Lorraine Elizabeth Baa died in California on November 4, 2021. She was 68.

Sources:

Judi Shimel, "Friends and Family Reflect on Lorraine Baa's Life and Legacy," https://stcroixsource.com/2021/11/02/friends-and-family-reflect-on-lorraine-baas-life-and-legacy/;

"Lorraine E. Baa," https://inforver.com/view/Lorraine-Baa-C5DNBd;

"Orlando Baa," https://www.myheritage.com/names/orlando_baa.

---

[62] Judi Shimel, "Friends and Family Reflect on Lorraine Baa's Life and Legacy," https://stcroixsource.com/2021/11/02/friends-and-family-reflect-on-lorraine-baas-life-and-legacy/.

"President's Corner: President Lorraine E. Baa," https://portal.clubrunner.ca/1579/Stories/president-s-corner-president-lorraine-e.-baa.

Monica Nieves Jacobs (1956-)

Image Ownership: Fair Usage

Lyric Soprano Monica Nieves Jacobs was born in 1956 and grew up in Christiansted, Virgin Islands and christened at St. John's Anglican Church where she began singing at an early age and later studying voice with Concert Pianists Stephen Bostic, Helen Francis Joseph, and Vocal Coach/Pianist William Lockwood Howcott.

A graduate of St. Croix Central High School, Jacobs has been the principal singer in numerous cantatas and a recitalist. She has performed with the St. Croix Inspirational Singers and has conducted choral ensembles on the islands, including the Deanery Choir and the Millennian Chorale.

Ingrid A. Bough (1959-)

Image Ownership: Fair Usage

Ingrid A. Bough, a Lyric Soprano, was born in Frederiksted, Virgin Islands, in 1959 to Violet Armstrong Bough,[63] an organist, and a public-school administrator.

Bough began singing in her church choir in Frederiksted at an early age. She studied privately with Rudy Schulterbrandt and Wesley Thomas. These studies continued throughout her high school years at St. Croix

---

[63] "On Island Profile: Ingrid A. Bough,"
https://stcroixsource.com/2006/01/10/island-profile-ingrid-bough/.

Central High School, where she played saxophone in the band.

Upon graduating from high school in 1977, Bough enrolled in Howard University in Washington, DC, where she majored in Music Education with principal instruments in voice and piano. She studied with the world-renowned opera singer Mattiwilda Dobbs and was a member of Howard's Choir under the baton of Dr. James Weldon Norris. Bough also performed as a soloist with Howard's Jazz Ensemble.

Bough returned to St. Croix and taught music for two years at John H. Woodson Junior High School.[64]

A member of the Alpha Kappa Alpha Sorority, Inc., Bough earned a Juris Doctorate from the University of Baltimore School of Law and a Master of Library & Information Science from the University of Maryland at College Park.[65]

In 2019, Ingrid A. Bough authored the book *Violet Loves the Letter "V": Virgin Islands Pride*.

Sources:

"Ingrid A. Bough, JD," https://outskirtspress.com/violetlovestheletterv;

"On Island Profile: Ingrid A. Bough," https://stcroixsource.com/2006/01/10/island-profile-ingrid-bough/.

---

[64] "On Island Profile: Ingrid A. Bough," https://stcroixsource.com/2006/01/10/island-profile-ingrid-bough/.
[65] " Ingrid A. Bough, JD," https://outskirtspress.com/violetlovestheletterv.

Denyce Graves (1964-)

Image Ownership: Fair Usage

Denyce Graves was born in Washington, DC, on March 7, 1964, to Charles Graves and Dorothy Middleton Graves-Kenner. A product of the DC Public School System, Graves graduated from the Duke Ellington School of the Arts in 1981. Afterward, she enrolled in the Oberlin Conservatory of Music in Oberlin, Ohio. However, she graduated from the New England Conservatory in Boston, Massachusetts, in 1985.[66]

n 1995, Graves made her operatic debut at the Metropolitan Opera in the title role of Georges Bizet's *Carmen*.[67] In 1999, Graves's plate was full as she performed the seductive role in Camille Saint-Saëns' Samson *et Dalila* with the Royal Opera, Covent Garden and The Washington Opera.[68]

In 2003, Denyce Graves became a Cultural Ambassador for the United States. In addition, she traveled to Poland,

---

[66] "Denyse Graves," https://peabody.jhu.edu/faculty/denyce-graves/.
[67] "Denyse Graves," https://peabody.jhu.edu/faculty/denyce-graves/
[68] "Denyse Graves," https://peabody.jhu.edu/faculty/denyce-graves.

Venezuela, and Romania for the State Department.[69] She teaches voice at the Peabody Conservatory of Music at Johns Hopkins in Baltimore, Maryland.[70]

Sources:

"Denyse Graves," https://peabody.jhu.edu/faculty/denyce-graves/;

Zuzanna Wisniewska, "Denyse Graves," https://www.blackpast.org/african-american-history/graves-denyce-1964/.

---

[69] Zuzanna Wisniewska, "Denyse Graves," https://www.blackpast.org/african-american-history/graves-denyce-1964/.
[70] Zuzanna Wisniewska, "Denyse Graves," https://www.blackpast.org/african-american-history/graves-denyce-1964/.

Audra Ann McDonald (1970-)

Image Ownership: Fair Usage

Audra Ann McDonald was born July 3, 1970, in West Berlin, Germany, to a military family, Stanley McDonald Jr. and Anna Kathryn, and grew up in Fresno, California. She graduated from Theodore Roosevelt High School in Fresno in 1986 and received the Bachelor of Music Performance degree in Voice from the Juilliard School for the Performing Arts in 1993.[71]

---

[71] Robert Viagas, "Grammy Winner Will Succeed Audra McDonald in Shuffle Along; Savion Glover Joining the Cast,"
https://www.playbill.com/article/grammy-winner-will-succeed-audra-mcdonald-in-shuffle-along-savion-glover-joining-the-cast.

In 1998, McDonald released her first solo album, *Way Back to Paradise*.

McDonald married actor Peter Donovan on September 10, 2000. However, their marriage was short-lived. In 2012, McDonald married actor William Swenson.

McDonald's operatic debut was in Francis Poulenc's *La voix humaine* in 2006 at the Houston Grand Opera. In 2007, she debuted with the Los Angeles Opera in the *Fall of the City of Mahagonny*.[72] In addition, she performed with the Boston Symphony, Chicago Symphony, Cleveland Orchestra, Los Angeles Philharmonic, New York Philharmonic, and San Francisco Symphony, to name a few.

A recipient of numerous awards, McDonald was awarded a Grammy Award for Best Classical Album and the Grammy Award for Best Opera Recording. And in 2016, she received the National Medal of Arts from President Barack Obama.[73]

Sources:

"Audra McDonald, Tony & Grammy Award Winner, Visits Saint Mary's College," https://www.saintmarys.edu/news-events/news-releases/audra-mcdonald-margaret-hill-visiting-artist-2013;

---

[72] "Audra McDonald, Tony & Grammy Award Winner, Visits Saint Mary's College," https://www.saintmarys.edu/news-events/news-releases/audra-mcdonald-margaret-hill-visiting-artist-2013.
[73] Ross McDonagh, "Heavily pregnant Audra McDonald, 46, receives National Medal of Arts - and a warm hug - from President Obama," https://www.dailymail.co.uk/tvshowbiz/article-3802670/Audra-McDonald-receives-National-Medal-Arts-warm-hug-President-Obama.html.

Robert Viagas, "Grammy Winner Will Succeed Audra McDonald in Shuffle Along; Savion Glover Joining the Cast," https://www.playbill.com/article/grammy-winner-will-succeed-audra-mcdonald-in-shuffle-along-savion-glover-joining-the-cast.

Ross McDonagh, "Heavily pregnant Audra McDonald, 46, receives National Medal of Arts - and a warm hug - from President Obama," https://www.dailymail.co.uk/tvshowbiz/article-3802670/Audra-McDonald-receives-National-Medal-Arts-warm-hug-President-Obama.html.

Arthur Petersen

Elizabeth Caballero (1974-)

Image Ownership: Fair Usage

Elizabeth Caballero was born in 1974 in Havana, Cuba,[74] to Jose Caballero and came to the United States as a child in the 1980 Mariel boat lift, the mass exodus from the Marxist-Leninist country. She was reared in Hialeah, Miami, Florida.[75] Caballero began piano studies as a child and went to study voice at Miami-Dade College. However, she received a Bachelor of Music in Vocal Performance from the University of Miami. In 2001, Caballero was a National Grand Finalist in the Metropolitan Opera National Council Auditions.[76]

---

[74] David Salazar, "From Refugee To Mimì – Soprano Elizabeth Caballero On Her Journey From Cuban Outcast to Opera Star," https://operawire.com/from-refugee-to-mimi-soprano-elizabeth-caballero-on-her-journey-from-cuban-outcast-to-opera-star/.
[75] "In the Park with Elizabeth Caballero," https://www.madisonopera.org/2018/07/06/in-the-park-with-elizabeth-caballero/.
[76] " Elizabeth Caballero, Soprano," https://venetianartssociety.org/events/elizabeth-caballero-soprano/

In 2009, Elizabeth Caballero made her Metropolitan Opera debut in Georges Bizet's *Carmen* as Frasquita.[77]

In 2012, Caballero portrayed Cio-Cio San in *Madama Butterfly* at the Lyric Opera of Kansas City, Missouri.[78] The same role was performed with Pensacola Opera in Pensacola, Florida.[79] In addition, she has performed as Mimi in La Bohème at the Staatsoper Stuttgart, and as Desdemona in *Otello* at the Palacio de Bellas Artes in Mexico City, and Teatro de la Zarzuela in Madrid, Spain singing the title role of Cecilia Valdés based on the novel by Cuban novelist Cirilo Villaverde.[80]

Elizabeth Caballero is the recipient of numerous awards, including the Diva Award from the New York City Opera and she was inducted into the Hall of Fame of Miami Dade College. In 2013, the University of Miami Frost School of Music presented her with the Distinguished Alumni Award.

Sources:

Biografías y Vidas, "Cirilo Villaverde," https://www.biografiasyvidas.com/biografia/v/villaverde.htm;

---

[77] The Metropolitan Opera, " Elizabeth Caballero, Soprano," https://www.metopera.org/discover/artists/soprano/elizabeth-caballero/.
[78] " Interviews, Editorials, Humour, Reviews, How-to Op Eds News," https://www.schmopera.com/talking-with-singers-elizabeth-caballero/.
[79] " Elizabeth Caballero, Soprano," https://venetianartssociety.org/events/elizabeth-caballero-soprano/.
[80] Biografías y Vidas, "Cirilo Villaverde," https://www.biografiasyvidas.com/biografia/v/villaverde.htm.

David Salazar, "From Refugee To Mimì – Soprano Elizabeth Caballero On Her Journey From Cuban Outcast to Opera Star," https://operawire.com/from-refugee-to-mimi-soprano-elizabeth-caballero-on-her-journey-from-cuban-outcast-to-opera-star/;

" Elizabeth Caballero, Soprano," https://venetianartssociety.org/events/elizabeth-caballero-soprano/;

"In the Park with Elizabeth Caballero," https://www.madisonopera.org/2018/07/06/in-the-park-with-elizabeth-caballero/;

Interviews, Editorials, Humour, Reviews, How-to Op Eds News," https://www.schmopera.com/talking-with-singers-elizabeth-caballero/;

The Metropolitan Opera, " Elizabeth Caballero, Soprano," https://www.metopera.org/discover/artists/soprano/elizabeth-caballero/.

Diamela del Pozo Pérez (1976-)

Image Ownership: Fair Usage

Mezzo-Soprano Diamela del Pozo Pérez was born on October 2, 1976, in Guantánamo, Cuba. She began singing at an early and plays the guitar as well as compose.[81]

In 1991, Pérez debuted in a local orchestra and in 1995, Pérez became a member of the female orchestra Son Damas in Havana.[82] She recorded two albums *Llegó Son Damas* (1997) and *A Todo Ritmo* (1999). She left Cuba in 2004.[83]

---

[81] "Diamela del Pozo Pérez," https://www.discogs.com/artist/4012296-Diamela-Del-Pozo.
[82] "Diamela del Pozo," https://music.metason.net/artistinfo?name=Diamela%20Del%20Pozo.
[83] "Diamela del Pozo Pérez," https://www.discogs.com/artist/4012296-Diamela-Del-Pozo.

Sources:

"Diamela del Pozo," https://music.metason.net/artistinfo?name=Diamela%20Del%20Pozo.

"Diamela del Pozo Pérez," https://www.discogs.com/artist/4012296-Diamela-Del-Pozo.

Pumeza Matshikiza (1979-)

Image Ownership: Fair Usage

Pumeza Matshikiza was born on February 27, 1979, in Lady Frere, South Africa. She graduated from the University of Cape Town College of Music and the Royal College of Music.[84]

In 2010, Matshikiza won the Veronica Dunne International Singing Competition in Dublin, Ireland. Afterward, she performed the role of Mimì in Giacomo Puccini's famous opera, La Bohème, at the Edinburgh Festival with Opera Bohemia. And in 2011, she became a member of the Stuttgart Opera in Germany. Other roles that Matshikiza

---

[84] "Pumeza Matshikiza," https://www.allmusic.com/artist/pumeza-matshikiza-mn0003143077/biography.

performed in Stuttgart included Ännchen in *Der Freischütz* and Pamina in *Die Zauberflöte*.[85]

In 2014, Matshikiza released her debut studio album, *Voice of Hope*, on the Decca Records label. During this year, she sang at the Commonwealth Games opening ceremony in Glasgow, Scotland.[86] In 2016, Pumeza Matshikiza released her second album, *Arias*.

Sources:

"Pumeza Matshikiza," https://www.allmusic.com/artist/pumeza-matshikiza-mn0003143077/biography;

"Pumeza Matshikiza," https://www.deccaclassics.com/en/artists/pumeza-matshikiza/news/biography-226774;

"Pumeza Matshikiza," https://vantunews.com/wiki/biography-pumeza-matshikiza.

---

[85] "Pumeza Matshikiza," https://www.deccaclassics.com/en/artists/pumeza-matshikiza/news/biography-226774.
[86] "Pumeza Matshikiza," https://www.deccaclassics.com/en/artists/pumeza-matshikiza/news/biography-226774.

Omo Bello (1982-)

Image Ownership: Fair Usage

Omo Bello was born in 1982 in Nigeria and in 2000, she graduated from Queen's College (a secondary school) in Lagos, Nigeria. Afterward, she enrolled in the University of Lagos, thus receiving a Bachelor of Science degree in Cell Biology and Genetics.[87]

In 2006 Bello left Nigeria to study music at École Normale de Musique de Paris, France. The following year in 2007, she was awarded a Diploma in music performance, went on to the Conservatoire de Paris, and obtained National University Diploma in Professional Music in 2009 She was

---

[87] "Omo Bello Musical Journey And Life In Brief," https://phamoxmusic.com/omo-bello/.

awarded 1st Prize at the Giovani Luciano Pavarotti Competition in Italy in 2010. She remained at the Conservatoire and earned a Master of Arts degree in voice 2011.[88] The following year, in 2012, Bello made her debut in Le Nozze di Figaro performing the role of Contessa at the Verbier Festival in Switzerland.[89]

Sources:

"Omo Bello Musical Journey And Life In Brief," https://phamoxmusic.com/omo-bello/.

"Omo Bello Musical Journey And Life In Brief," https://phamoxmusic.com/omo-bello/.

"Omo Bello," http://www.omobello.com/about.html.

Onika Michelle Thomas (1984-)

Image Ownership: Fair Usage

Onika Michelle Thomas was born on April 7, 1984, in Christiansted, Virgin Islands, to Maurice McKenzie Thomas, a public-school administrator from Christiansted, and Monica Maria Thomas, an elementary school teacher from Trinidad, West Indies.

At the age of two, Thomas began dance studies with Street Theatre Dance, and by 11, her piano studies began with William Lockwood Howcott. She continued these art activities, added voice, and became a member of Saint Croix Central High School Mixed Concert Choir, Madrigal

Singers, and Captain of the Music Auxiliary Dance Team. Thomas graduated with honors in 2001. Afterward, she was offered a full scholarship to Lincoln University of Pennsylvania, where she graduated summa cum Laude in philosophy and music in 2005.[90]

While at Lincoln, Thomas studied voice during the summers in Washington, DC, with Charlotte Wesley Holloman and Nelda Ormond at the University of the District of Columbia. She also studied piano with Geraldine Hayslett Thomas Boone in Norfolk, Virginia.[91]

As a recitalist and interpreter of German Lieder and American Art Songs, Thomas performed throughout the eastern corridor of the United States- New Jersey, Washington, DC, Virginia, and the Virgin Islands.

Sources:

"On Island Profile: Onika Michelle Thomas," https://stthomassource.com/content/2005/07/13/island-profile-onika-michelle-thomas/;

Otis D Alexander, *One Drop of Imagination: Embracing Selected Arts Energies* ((New York: African Tree Press, 2019).

---

[90] "On Island Profile: Onika Michelle Thomas," https://stthomassource.com/content/2005/07/13/island-profile-onika-michelle-thomas/.
[91] Otis D Alexander, One Drop of Imagination: Embracing Selected Arts Energies ((New York: African Tree Press, 2019).

Angel Joy Blue (1984-)

Image Ownership: Fair Usage

Angel Joy Blue was born on May 3, 1984, in Los Angeles, California, to Sylvester Blue. She graduated from Los Angeles County High School for the Arts in 2001.[92]

In 2005, Blue received a Bachelor of Music from the University of Redlands and a Master of Music degree in Opera Performance from the University of California at Los Angeles in 2007.

Blue debuted in Frankfurt, Germany as the 3rd Norn in Richard Wagner's *Götterdämmerung* in 2010.[93] In 2018, Blue performed the role of the young slave girl Liù in

---

[92] "Angel Joy Blue," https://www.imdb.com/name/nm7554879/bio.
[93] "Angel Blue," https://www.angeljoyblue.com/?q=AboutAngel.

Turandot with the San Diego Opera.[94] The following year, 2019, she performed the principal role in George Gershwin's *Porgy and Bess* with the New York Metropolitan Opera.[95] Blue won the Grammy Award for Best Opera Recording for the Metropolitan Opera production of Porgy and Bess in the 63rd Annual Grammy Awards in 2021.[96]

Sources:

"Alumna Angel Joy Blue returns to UCLA to perform on Nov. 21," https://newsroom.ucla.edu/releases/alumna-angel-joy-blue-returns-to-ucla-to-perform-on-nov-21;

"Angel Blue," https://www.angeljoyblue.com/?q=AboutAngel.

"Angel Joy Blue," https://www.imdb.com/name/nm7554879/bio.

Eva Cahen, "Sitting down with Angel Joy Blue," http://www.operavivra.com/articles/interviews/sitting-down-with-angel-joy-blue/;

Grammy Awards, "Angel Blue," https://www.grammy.com/artists/angel-blue/287143.

---

[94] Eva Cahen, "Sitting down with Angel Joy Blue," http://www.operavivra.com/articles/interviews/sitting-down-with-angel-joy-blue/.
[95] "Alumna Angel Joy Blue returns to UCLA to perform on Nov. 21," https://newsroom.ucla.edu/releases/alumna-angel-joy-blue-returns-to-ucla-to-perform-on-nov-21.
[96] Grammy Awards, "Angel Blue," https://www.grammy.com/artists/angel-blue/287143.

Pretty Yende (1985-)

Pretty Yende was born in Piet Retief, South Africa, on March 6, 1985, and made her operatic debut at the Latvian National Theatre in Riga, Latvia, as Micaela in Georges Bizet's *Carmen*. In 2010 and 2011, she performed Berenice in *L'occasione fa il ladro* and Elvira in *L'italiana*, respectively, at La Scala, Italy. She is a 2011 graduate of the Young Artists Accademia of the Teatro alla Scala.[97]

In 2013, Yende made her New York Metropolitan Opera debut in the role of Adèle in Gioachino Rossini's *Le comte*

---

[97] "Pretty Yende," https://prettyyende.com/biography/.

Ory.⁹⁸ In 2016, she made history by being the first Black soprano to play the role of Lucia di Lammermoor by Gaetano Donizetti at thin e Paris Opera, and 2019, Pretty Yende became a Knight of the Order of the Star of Italy, an Italian order of chivalry, and was reformed from the Order of the Star of Italian Solidarity by Giorgio Napolitano, the 11th President of Italy.⁹⁹ Pretty Yende performed La Sonnambula opera at the Théâtre des Champs-Elysées in Paris in 2021.¹⁰⁰

Sources:

Mary von Aue, "Pretty Yende Is Opera's New Star, But She Wants to Talk About Fear," https://observer.com/2019/03/pretty-yende-opera-new-star-talks-fear-humility-rejection/;

"Pretty Yende," https://prettyyende.com/biography/;

"SA Opera Singer Pretty Yende in Shocking Encounter with Paris Police," https://www.sapeople.com/2021/06/22/sa-opera-singer-pretty-yende-suffers-paris-airport-nightmare-with-alleged-police-racism/.

---

⁹⁸ Mary von Aue, "Pretty Yende Is Opera's New Star, But She Wants to Talk About Fear," https://observer.com/2019/03/pretty-yende-opera-new-star-talks-fear-humility-rejection/.
⁹⁹"SA Opera Singer Pretty Yende in Shocking Encounter with Paris Police," https://www.sapeople.com/2021/06/22/sa-opera-singer-pretty-yende-suffers-paris-airport-nightmare-with-alleged-police-racism/.
¹⁰⁰ "SA Opera Singer Pretty Yende in Shocking Encounter with Paris Police," https://www.sapeople.com/2021/06/22/sa-opera-singer-pretty-yende-suffers-paris-airport-nightmare-with-alleged-police-racism/.

J'Nai Bridges (1987)

Image Ownership: Fair Usage

J'Nai Bridges was born in 1987 and was reared in Lakewood, Washington. She is a 2005 graduate of the Charles Wright Academy in Tacoma. She received a Bachelor of Music degree in vocal performance from the Manhattan School of Music in New York and earned a Master of Music degree from the Curtis Institute of Music in Philadelphia, Pennsylvania.[101] In 2012, Bridges won the "Prize of the Public" at Operalia, The World Opera Competition, and the Marian Anderson Award. In 2015, Bridges premiered the role of Carmen in the opera *Bel Canto* with the Lyric Opera of Chicago. The following year

---

[101] "American mezzo-soprano J'Nai Bridges, known for her "rich, dark, exciting sound" (Opera News) is quickly becoming one of the most sought-after talents of her generation," https://jnaibridgesmezzo.com/biography/.

in 2016, she performed the role of Nefertiti in Philip Glass' *Akhnaten* with the Los Angeles Opera. And in 2019, she performed the title role in Georges Bizet's Carmen with the San Francisco Opera. In Glass' work, Bridges won Best Opera Recording at the 64th Grammy Award in 2022.[102]

Sources:

"American mezzo-soprano J'Nai Bridges, known for her "rich, dark, exciting sound" (Opera News) is quickly becoming one of the most sought-after talents of her generation," https://jnaibridgesmezzo.com/biography/.

"J'Nai wins Grammy Award for "Akhnaten," https://jnaibridgesmezzo.com/2022/04/04/jnai-wins-grammy-award-for-akhnaten;

"Review: A Singer Brings Her Splendid Sound to an Eclectic Recital," https://www.nytimes.com/2022/12/02/arts/music/jnai-bridges-recital-review.html.

---

[102] "J'Nai wins Grammy Award for "Akhnaten," https://jnaibridgesmezzo.com/2022/04/04/jnai-wins-grammy-award-for-akhnaten.

Yolisa Ngwexana

Image Ownership: Fair Usage

Yolisa Ngwexana, soprano, was born in Cofimvaba, South Africa. However, there was no information provided about any of their ages. In 2015, Ngwexana won the Western Cape Choral Music Association soloist development competition. The following year in 2016, Ngwexana performed with the chorus of Cape Town Opera in George's Bizet's Carmen; in 2017, she was a soloist for the KwaZulu-Natal Philharmonic Orchestra Youth Concerto Festival.

Ngwexana received a Diploma in Biotechnology at the Cape Peninsula University of Technology and studied music at North-West University in Potchefstroom, South Africa.

In 2019 Ngwexana won second place in the Mimi Coertse Scholarship Competition, and in 2020 she was a category winner in The Voices of South Africa Opera Singing Competition.

In 2020 Ngwexana made her debut as Lauretta in Puccini's Gianni Schicchi with the South Africa Operatunity company in Cape Town.

Sources:

David Salazar, "The Voice of Black Opera Competition Announces 12 Semifinalists,"https://operawire.com/the-voice-of-black-opera-competition-announces-12-semifinalists/;

Delicious Divas, https://footnotes.co.za/delicious-divas/;

"Yolisa Ngwexana,"https://joziopera.co.za/our-people/yolisa-ngwexana/;

Khayakazi Madlala

Image Ownership: Fair Usage

Khayakazi Madlala, soprano, was born in Matatiele, South Africa, and sang at an age under the tutelage of her brother Sindani Gecelo. She attended Mariazell high school and studied music further at North-West University in Potchefstroom. She has performed for Gauteng Operas in Ferreirasdorp at the Durban Playhouse. She has performed at the Mälmo Opera House in Sweden. In 2015, Khayakazi was part of the Gauteng Opera ad hoc chorus in Ferreirasdorp. In 2017, she performed the role of Mimi in the Gauteng Opera production of La Bohème at the Joburg Theatre and The Playhouse in Durban. In addition, Madlala won 3rd place in The Voices of South Africa Opera Singing Competition in 2020.

Sources:

"Aardklop Aubade Presents "Delicious Divas, A Concert of Operatic Gems," https://bsharp-entertainment.com/aardklop-aubade-presents-delicious-divas-a-concert-of-operatic-gems/;

"Inaugural Opera for Peace Prize at the "Voices of South Africa International Singing Competition 2020,"https://operaforpeace.org/news/inaugural-opera-for-peace-prize-at-the-voices-of-south-africa-international-competition-2020;

"Gauteng Opera presents Giacomo Puccini's La bohème,"https://creativefeel.co.za/2017/06/gauteng-opera-presents-giacomo-puccinis-la-boheme/.

I Paved the Way

Other Up and coming South African Opera Singers

Natasha Agarwal, Isabelle Peters, Rachel Duckett, Suzanna Taffot, Nosipho Majola, Lindiwe Lebakeng, Nontsikelelo Mnegela, Samkelisiwe Sitshinga, Chantelle Grant, Shanice Skinner, and Lebogang Polori.

Source:

Florence Lockheart, "Voice of Black Opera Competition Returns to Birmingham,"https://www.classical-music.uk/news/article/voice-of-black-opera-competition-returns-to-birmingham.

Venessa van der Westhuizen, "Outstanding performances by NWU students at international opera singing competition,"https://potchefstroomherald.co.za/75886/outstanding-performances-by-nwu-students-at-international-opera-singing-competition/amp.

Arthur Petersen
Part II: **PIANISTS**

Catalina Berroa Ojea (1849-1911)

Catalina Berroa Ojea, composer, singer, and pianist, was born on February 28, 1849, in Trinidad, Las Villas, Cuba.[103] She was the principal organist in the Iglesia San Francisco de Assis, organist/choirmaster of Iglesia de la Santissima Trinidad, she founded a music academy in Trinidad.[104]

In addition to being a pianist, Ojea performed on the cello in a trio with Manuel Jimenez on violin and Ana Luisa Vivanco on piano. Ojea was the principal violinist of the Brunet Theater orchestra.[105]

Ojea's compositions include:
"Song The Trinity," 1867; "Song, Song of Belisa and Josefa," 1902; "Conchita March," "May Flowers Church Music, for horn and piano," "The Virgin of Cuba, for chorus," and "Save for two voices, voice, and organ.[106]
Catalina Berroa Ojea, Cuba's first female conductor, died on November 23, 1911. She was 62.

---

[103] "Catalina Berroa," https://www.howold.co/person/catalina-berroa.
[104] "Berroa Ojea, Catalina," "https://composers-classical-music.com/b/BerroaCatalina.htm.
[105] "Catalina Berroa," https://prabook.com/web/catalina.berroa/2490902.
[106] "Berroa Ojea, Catalina," "https://composers-classical-music.com/b/BerroaCatalina.htm.

Sources:

"Berroa Ojea, Catalina," "https://composers-classical-music.com/b/BerroaCatalina.htm.

"Catalina Berroa," https://www.howold.co/person/catalina-berroa;
"Catalina Berroa," https://prabook.com/web/catalina.berroa/2490902.

Arthur Petersen
Carmen Velma Shepperd (1910-1997)

Image Ownership: Fair Usage

Carmen Velma Shepperd was born on October 30, 1910, in Kingston, Jamaica, to David N. Shepperd and Theresa Ann Rodriquez Shepperd. However, Carmen grew up in Harlem, New York. Her music studies on the piano began at six.

Shepperd graduated from the Wadleigh High School for Girls in New York City in 1928. Afterward, she enrolled in the Piano Performance Diploma program at the Damrosch Institute/ Juilliard School of Music. In 1930, she created the Carmen Shepperd School of Music in Harlem and was awarded a service medal in 1931 by the New York Music Week Association at Carnegie Hall. [107]

Shepperd graduated from Damrosch Institute with a Piano diploma in 1932 and a voice and performance diploma in 1934.[108] Two years later, in 1936, In Sheppard received a Bachelor of Music degree from Columbia University Department of Music and earned a Master of Music Education degree from Teachers College.

From 1947 to 1948, Shepperd studied opera 1947 at École des Beaux-Arts in Fontainebleau, France.

Carmen Velma Shepperd, a member of Delta sigma Theta Sorority, Inc.,[109] died in Brooklyn, New York, on December 6, 1997. She was 87.

Sources:

"Carmen Velma Shepperd Explained," https://everything.explained.today/Carmen_Velma_Shepperd/.

---

[107] "Carmen Velma Shepperd Explained," https://everything.explained.today/Carmen_Velma_Shepperd/.
[108] Lucien H. White, "Carmen Velma Shepperd Graduates in Singing from Damrosch Institute," https://www.newspapers.com/clip/72178121/carmen-velma-shepperd-graduates-in.
[109] "Carmen Velma Shepperd Explained," https://everything.explained.today/Carmen_Velma_Shepperd/.

Lucien H. White, "Carmen Velma Shepperd Graduates in Singing from Damrosch Institute," https://www.newspapers.com/clip/72178121/carmen-velma-shepperd-graduates.

I Paved the Way
Sylvia Olden Lee (1917 –2004)

Image Ownership: Fair Usage

Sylvia Olden Lee, a vocal coach, pianist, accompanist, was born on June 29, 1917, in Meridian, Mississippi, to James Olden, a Minister, and Sylvia Ward. Both parents were graduates of the HBCU Fisk University.[110] After high school, Lee enrolled in Howard University School of Music in Washington, DC, majoring in piano, organ, and voice. She later transferred to the Oberlin Conservatory of Music in Oberlin, Ohio.

---

[110] "Tribute to Sylvia Olden Lee, Master Musician and Teacher," https://larouchepub.com/other/2017/4426tribute_sylvia.html.

In 1933, Lee performed on piano at the White House for the inauguration of Franklin Delano Roosevelt and toured with Bass-Baritone Paul Robeson in 1942.[111]

In 1944, Sylvia married the renowned conductor, and violinist Everett Lee from Wheeling, West Virginia. They parented two children, Everett Lee, III, and Dr. Eve Lee.[112]

The Metropolitan Opera hired Lee as a vocal coach in 1954, making her the first African American to hold such a position. Before Lee's offer, her mother had also been offered a role. However, she refused because they did not want her to tell people that she was black.

Lee taught at the famous Curtis Institute of Music in Philadelphia, Pennsylvania. She also taught at Talladega College in Alabama, Dillard University in Louisiana, and Howard University[113] where she coached Jessye Norman and Kathleen Battle.

Sylvia Olden Lee died on April 10, 2004. She was 87.

Sources:

"Everett Lee, First African-American to Conduct on Broadway, Has Died at 105," https://theviolinchannel.com/everett-lee-the-first-african-american-to-conduct-on-broadway-has-died-aged-105/.

---

[111] "Sylvia Lee: Coach, Master," https://prabook.com/web/sylvia.lee/1836410.
[112] "Everett Lee, First African-American to Conduct on Broadway, Has Died at 105," https://theviolinchannel.com/everett-lee-the-first-african-american-to-conduct-on-broadway-has-died-aged-105/.
[113] "Tribute to Sylvia Olden Lee, Master Musician and Teacher," https://larouchepub.com/other/2017/4426tribute_sylvia.html.

"Sylvia Lee: Coach, Master," https://prabook.com/web/sylvia.lee/1836410;

"Tribute to Sylvia Olden Lee, Master Musician and Teacher," https://larouchepub.com/other/2017/4426tribute_sylvia.html.

Arthur Petersen
Hazel Dorothy Scott (1920-1981)

Image Ownership: Fair Usage

Hazels Dorothy Scott, a classical, jazz, and boogie-woogie blues stylist was born in Port of Spain, Trinidad, on June 11, 1920.[114] However, Scott was reared in Harlem, New York. An only child of R. Thomas Scott, a West African educator, and Alma Long Scott, a classically trained pianist and saxophonist, Hazel was playing by ear very early and had perfect pitch. At eight, Scott auditioned for the Juilliard School of Music, performing a variation of Sergei Rachmaninoff's "Prelude in C-Sharp Minor." Scott was awarded a scholarship from the audition to study there privately with Piano Professor Oscar Wagner. And by 13,

---

[114] "Hazel Scott," https://www.womenshistory.org/education-resources/biographies/hazel-scott.

she was performing professionally with her mother's jazz band, Alma Long Scott's American Creolians.[115]

In 1938, at 18, Scott made her Broadway debut in the musical revue Sing Out the News and still was able to graduate from high school with high honors. And in 1940, Scott performed a classical recital at Carnegie Hall in New York.[116]

In addition to playing piano recitals, Scott performed in five Hollywood films, including *I Dood It* in 1943 and *Broadway Rhythm* in 1944.[117] In 1945, Scott married Adam Clayton Powell, Jr., the first elected African American Congress from New York. The following year in 1946, they became the parents of a son, Adam Clayton Powell III.[118] Four years later, in 1950, Scott had her television show, The Hazel Scott Show, thus making her the first African American woman to host an artistic presentation during Jim Crow. Scott played the mix she was known for, and the show earned good ratings. Scott's show was canceled because she was sympathetic to the communist. However, she moved to Paris, France, in 1957 and did become a member of the Black expatriate community.[119]

---

[115] "Hazel Scott," https://www.womenshistory.org/education-resources/biographies/hazel-scott.
[116] Maddy Shaw Roberts, "Who was Hazel Scott, the forgotten jazz virtuoso who fought against racial segregation?" https://amp.classicfm.com/discover-music/instruments/piano/hazel-scott-jazz-entertainer-fought-racial-segregation/.
[117] Maddy Shaw Roberts, "Who was Hazel Scott, the forgotten jazz virtuoso who fought against racial segregation?" https://amp.classicfm.com/discover-music/instruments/piano/hazel-scott-jazz-entertainer-fought-racial-segregation/
[118] "Hazel Scott," https://www.smithsonianmag.com/arts-culture/hazel-scotts-lifetime-of-high-notes-145939027/.
[119] "Who's Hazel Scott? (Unsung Women of Jazz #11)," https://curtjazz.com/2019/02/20/whos-hazel-scott-unsung-women-of-jazz-11-2/.

Hazels Dorothy Scott, a piano virtuoso, died in New York City on October 2, 1981. She was 61.

Sources:

"Hazel Scott," https://www.womenshistory.org/education-resources/biographies/hazel-scott;

"Hazel Scott," https://www.smithsonianmag.com/arts-culture/hazel-scotts-lifetime-of-high-notes-145939027/.

Maddy Shaw Roberts, "Who was Hazel Scott, the forgotten jazz virtuoso who fought against racial segregation?" https://amp.classicfm.com/discover-music/instruments/piano/hazel-scott-jazz-entertainer-fought-racial-segregation/;

"Who's Hazel Scott? (Unsung Women of Jazz #11)," https://curtjazz.com/2019/02/20/whos-hazel-scott-unsung-women-of-jazz-11-2/.

I Paved the Way
Helen I. Francis Joseph (1921-2020)

Image Ownership: Fair Usage

Helen I. Francis Joseph, pianist, organist, vocal coach, conductor, and educator was born in Christiansted, Virgin Islands, in 1921. She began piano studies at the age of five. By the time she was 10, Joseph was performing a full-length recital, accompanying musicians, and playing for churches.

Joseph graduated from Hampton Institute, now Hampton University, where she majored in education and music.

Upon returning to the Virgin Islands after her studies, Joseph was a classroom teacher, pianist, and organist/choral conductor for several churches, including St. John's Anglican Church and the Moravian Church, Friedensfeld.

Joseph retired from the Virgin Islands Department of Education as a school principal.

Joseph performed classical recitals throughout the entire Virgin Islands, including at the Whim Great House Museum and Island Center for the Performing Arts, to name a few venues. In addition, she was an accompanist for the St. Croix Central High School Mixed Choir and was always seen in the Crucian Christmas Fiesta performing with the renowned band Stanley & the Ten Sleepless Knights.

Helen I. Francis Joseph, who had one daughter, Fern Joseph McAlpin, died on April 19, 2020, in St. Croix, Virgin Islands. She was 91.[120]

Sources:

"Helen I. Joseph Dies at 91," https://stthomassource.com/content/2020/05/04/helen-i-joseph-dies-at-91/.

Jeanette Hayslett Wallace (1930-2017)

Image Ownership: Fair Usage

Jeanette Hayslett Wallace, pianist, organist, recitalist was born on February 19, 1930 in Norfolk County, Virginia to John Hayslett and Mattie Hayslett.[121] Jeanette graduated from Virginia State College (now University) in Petersburg, Virginia. She was a music teacher for 37 years with the City of Chesapeake and a member of First Baptist Church, Berkley, Tidewater Area Musicians Branch of the National Association of Negro Musicians, and Delta Sigma Theta Sorority, Inc.[122] Jeanette was married to Clarence Wallace. They parented Clarence Michael Wallace and Charnette Wallace Simmons.

---

[121] "Jeanette Hayslett Wallace," https://www.pretlowandsons.com/obituary/4073403

[122] "Edwards, Pearly Hayslett, Geraldine Hayslett Boone, and Jeanette Wallace, 1980, 1995," https://archives.lib.duke.edu/catalog/behindtheveil_aspace_1102fddb-2c64-4077-8455-604e2f0a6008;

Jeanette Hayslett Wallace died on January 15, 2017. She was 87.

Sources:

"Edwards, Pearly Hayslett, Geraldine Hayslett Boone, and Jeanette Wallace, 1980, 1995," https://archives.lib.duke.edu/catalog/behindtheveil_aspace_1102fddb-2c64-4077-8455-604e2f0a6008;

"Jeanette Hayslett Wallace," https://www.pretlowandsons.com/obituary/4073403.

Nina Simone (1933-2003)

Nina Simone was a nickname name given to her by a boyfriend, and for the French actress Simone Signoret; respectively was born Eunice Kathleen Waymon in Tryon, North Carolina, on February 21, 1933,[123] to John Divine Waymon, an entertainer and barber, and Mary Kate Irvin Waymon, a Methodist minister. She had one brother, Sam Waymon, a Musical composer, pianist, and vocalist.

She began playing piano by ear at the age of three. And by six, Simone started classical music with Muriel Mazzanovich, an Englishwoman who had moved to Tryon

---

[123] "Her Story: Nina Simone," http://shemadehistory.com/her-story-nina-simone/.

and introduced her to the works of Johann Sebastian Bach and Frédéric Chopin.

Simone graduated valedictorian of the Allen High School for Girls, a private, integrated high school in Asheville, North Carolina, in 1950 and was ready to study at the Juilliard School in New York City. The community raised money for a scholarship to assist her with her goal as a gifted and talented girl. However, Simone wanted to study classical piano at the prestigious Curtis Institute of Music in Philadelphia, Pennsylvania.[124] However, she was rejected in 1951 because of her skin color.

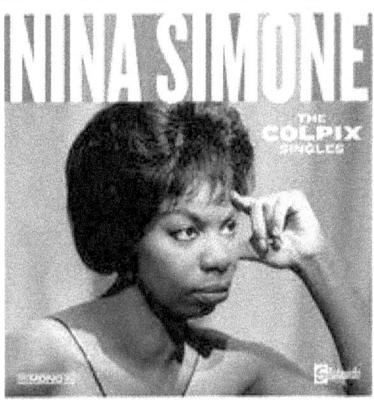

In 1954, Simone began playing piano and singing at the Midtown Bar and Grill in Atlantic City, New Jersey. In 1958, she released her debut album, Little Girl Blue, with Bethlehem Records.[125] The following year, 1959, Simone's version of "I Love You, Porgy" from George Gershwin's opera Porgy and Bess became Simone's only single Billboard Top 20 chart hit in the United States.

---

[124] Mariana Brandman, "Nina Simone," https://www.ninasimone.com/biography/.
[125] Lisa Torem, "Nina Simone - Nina Simone," https://pennyblackmusic.co.uk/Home/DetailsMobile?id=21081.

In 1965, when playwright Lorraine Hansberry's ('Raisin in the Sun') early death prevented her from completing 'To Be Young, Gifted and Black,' Simone took it upon herself to bring closure to work by composing an anthemic original song.[126]

Simone's song of protest, Mississippi Goddam," which was composed four years earlier regarding the bombing of the church in Birmingham, Alabama, and the assassination of Medgar Evers, was performed again in 1968, three days after the assassination of Dr. Martin Luther King, Jr. Afterward, she came out with songs like "The King of Love is Dead," "Do What You Gotta Do," and the cover on the piano score "You'll Never Walk Alone."
And she recorded more than 40 albums.

Simone received four career Grammy Award nominations, two while on earth, and the others were awarded posthumously.[127]

In 2003, the Curtis Institute of Music awarded Simone an Honorary Doctor degree in Music and Humanities. Nina Simone died on April 21, 2003, Carry-le-Rouet, France, two days after she was honored by the Curtis. She was 70.
2018 Nina Simone was inducted into the Rock and Roll Hall of Fame 2018.

---

[126] "Nina Simone's 'Lovely, Precious Dream' For Black Children," https://www.npr.org/2019/01/08/683021559/nina-simone-to-be-young-gifted-and-black-american-anthem.
[127] "Her Story: Nina Simone,"http://shemadehistory.com/her-story-nina-simone/.

Sources:

"Her Story: Nina Simone," http://shemadehistory.com/her-story-nina-simone/;

Lisa Torem, "Nina Simone - Nina Simone," https://pennyblackmusic.co.uk/Home/DetailsMobile?id=21081;

Mariana Brandman, "Nina Simone," https://www.ninasimone.com/biography/;

"Nina Simone's 'Lovely, Precious Dream' For Black Children," https://www.npr.org/2019/01/08/683021559/nina-simone-to-be-young-gifted-and-black-american-anthem.

I Paved the Way
Geraldine Hayslett Thomas Boone (1936-)

Image Ownership: Fair Usage

Concert pianist, organist, composer, and conductor Geraldine Hayslett Thomas Boone, was born in Norfolk County, Virginia on January 7, 1936 to John Hayslett and Mattie Hayslett. Geraldine received a Bachelor of Arts degree from Virginia State College (now University) in 1958 and earned a Master of Music degree in Music Theory from the Eastman School of Music at the University of Rochester in Rochester, New York.[128]

The founder of the Boy Choir of Hampton Roads and the Chesapeake Civic Chorus in 1986, Boone a past vice president of the National Association of Negro Musicians, Inc. Boone taught at the Governors School for the Arts and was the piano accompanist for Norfolk Academy School Chorus. In 1993, Boone e retired from the Norfolk Public

---

[128] "Edwards, Pearly Hayslett, Geraldine Hayslett Boone, and Jeanette Wallace, 1980, 1995,"
https://archives.lib.duke.edu/catalog/behindtheveil_aspace_1102fddb-2c64-4077-8455-604e2f0a6008.

School System as a Music Teacher and taught theory and composition at Norfolk State University School of Music.[129] Geraldine Hayslett Thomas Boone is a member of the Alpha Kappa Alpha Sorority, Inc.

Sources:

"Edwards, Pearly Hayslett, Geraldine Hayslett Boone, and Jeanette Wallace, 1980, 1995," https://archives.lib.duke.edu/catalog/behindtheveil_aspace_1102fddb-2c64-4077-8455-604e2f0a6008;

New Journal & Guide, "Social And Civic Whirl: Mrs. Geraldine T. Boone Receives The Roland Carter Living Legends In Church Music Honor," https://thenewjournalandguide.com/social-civic-whirl-mrs-geraldine-t-boone-receives-roland-carter-living-legends-church-music-honor/.

---

[129] New Journal & Guide, "Social And Civic Whirl: Mrs. Geraldine T. Boone Receives The Roland Carter Living Legends In Church Music Honor," https://thenewjournalandguide.com/social-civic-whirl-mrs-geraldine-t-boone-receives-roland-carter-living-legends-church-music-honor/.

Phyllis King Leach

Image Ownership: Fair Usage

Phyllis King Leach was born in St. John, Antigua, and began piano and art studies there. She became the organist at the Episcopal Church during her high school years. After graduating, Leach left the island for New York City to enroll in Barnard College, where she majored in Latin and minored in music performance. During her tenure at Barnard, Leach was invited to perform solo with the Columbia University Symphony Orchestra.

After graduating from Barnard, Leach traveled to Chicago, where she earned a Master of Arts degree from Northwestern University and continued to concertize as a pianist.

Leached retired as an educator in the 1980s and relocated to the island of St. Croix, accepting a position as Organist/Choir Director of St. Paul's Anglican Church in Frederiksted. She also taught music at St. Dunstan's Episcopal School in Christiansted. She continued concertizing at the Whim Great House Museum "Candlelight Concerts," Island Center for the Performing Arts, and accompanying the St. Croix Central High School Concert Choix and Chamber Ensemble for International Competitions in New York, Atlanta, Georgia, and Virginia.

I Paved the Way
Hildred Elizabeth Roach (1937-)

Image Ownership: Fair Usage

Hildred Elizabeth Roach, pianist, was born on June 1, 1937, in Charlotte, North Carolina.[130] She received a Bachelor of Arts degree in Piano from Fisk University in Nashville, Tennessee, in 1958 and earned a Master of Music in Piano and Theory from Yale University. Her postgraduate studies include the Juilliard School, the University of Ghana, and Oakland University.

A recitalist and music historian, Roach has taught at Fayetteville State University, Howard University, Tuskegee University, and Virginia State University and retired as a full professor at the University of the District of

---

[130] "Hildred E. Roach," https://www.officialusa.com/names/Hildred-Roach.

Columbia. She was married to Attorney James L. Stafford.[131]

Hildred Elizabeth Roach is the author of *Black American Music: Past and Present: Pan-African Composers Thenceforth and Now.*

Sources:

"Hildred E. Roach," https://www.officialusa.com/names/Hildred-Roach;

"James L. Stafford," https://www.legacy.com/us/obituaries/washingtonpost/name/james-stafford-obituary?id=5514046.

---

[131] "James L. Stafford," https://www.legacy.com/us/obituaries/washingtonpost/name/james-stafford-obituary?id=5514046.

I Paved the Way

Philippa Smith Tyler (1946-)

Image Ownership: Fair Usage

Philippa Smith Tyler, pianist, conductor, and educator was born in Washington, DC in 1946. To be sure, her mother, Catherine Atkinson Smith, an opera composer, was her first piano teacher. She began piano studies at an early age.

After high school, Smith Tyler enrolled in Howard University in Washington, where she majored in piano. While there, she was also the accompanist for Jessye Norman, who later became a renowned opera singer.

Smith Tyler later transferred to the New England Conservatory of Music in Boston, Massachusetts, and received the Bachelor of Music degree in piano. In addition, Smith Tyler has studied at the American University and George Washington University in Washington, DC, and the Westminster Choir College in Pennsylvania.

Smith Tyler has performed widely throughout the United States and the Republic of Cuba. She has also taught piano at the University of the District of Columbia.

Philippa Smith Tyler is Organist/Choir Director at St. Paul's Anglican Church in Frederiksted, Virgin Islands.

Adele Darlene Allen (1953-)

Image Ownership: Fair Usage

Adele Darlene Allen, the concert pianist, organist, and conductor, physician was born March 19, 1953, in Brooklyn, New York, to Dr. Oscar Clement Allen and Hattie Lawson Allen, a registered nurse, school administrator, and author from Danville, Virginia. She has one sister, Carol Allen, a physician.

At age 5, Allen began piano studies and continued with David LeVita, a musicologist at the Brooklyn Museum. Allen graduated from Midwood High School in Brooklyn. She received a Bachelor of Arts degree in Economics and Political Science and a minor in Piano Performance from

Wellesley College in Wellesley, Massachusetts, in 1973, where she founded the African American Gospel Choir.[132]

After leaving Wellesley, Allen studied organ at the New York School of Liturgical Music and the New England Conservatory of Music in Boston, Massachusetts.

Wanting to fulfill her dream as a physician, Allen received a Master of Science degree in Human Nutrition from Columbia University College of Physicians & Surgeons Institute of Human Nutrition. In 1985, she earned a Doctor of Medicine degree from the American University of the Caribbean School of Medicine in Plymouth, Montserrat.[133]

Allen has performed at the Whim Great House Museum "Candlelight Concerts" in Frederiksted, Virgin Islands, and conducted many ensembles, including members of the El Conservatorio de Música de Puerto Rico, and performed classical compositions with the Polymnia Chorus and the Puerto Rico Symphony Chamber Orchestra at Saints Peter and Paul Cathedral in Charlotte Amalie, Virgin Islands. Also, she has accompanied Austin A. Venzen, the New York Symphony Orchestra flutist, and opera baritone Lawrence O. Benjamin, as well as the Saint Croix Central High School Mixed Ensemble during its international competitions in New York, Atlanta, and Virginia Beach, Virginia.

A member of Alpha Kappa Alpha Sorority, Inc, Dr. Allen released the CD *Out of the Black Experience* in 2009.

---

[132] "Adele's World of Music: Classical and Modern Music," https://adelesworldofmusic.webs.com/.
[133] "Adele Allen," https://www.linkedin.com/in/adele-allen-m-d-42b77614/.

Sources:

"Adele Allen,"https://www.linkedin.com/in/adele-allen-m-d-42b77614/;

"Adele's World of Music: Classical and Modern Music," https://adelesworldofmusic.webs.com/.

Arthur Petersen
Barbara Gene Forde Browne (1956-)

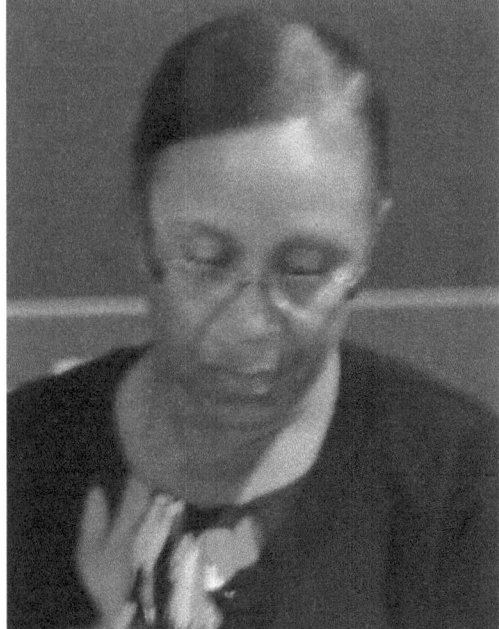

Image Ownership: Fair Usage

Concert Pianist, accompanist, and conductor Barbara-Gene Forde Browne was born in May 1956 in Boston, Massachusetts, to Joyce Barbara Shannon Forde, an educator from Guyana, and Pastor Kenneth Eugene Forde, from St. Andrew Barbados. Browne has two siblings, Joyce Darlene Forde Alexander and Dianne Forde

Richardson.

Photography by Ralph Burgess
Barbara-Gene Browne at the piano with Saint Croix Central High School Mixed Chorus at the North American Music Festival in Virginia Beach.

Browne began piano studies at an early age and continued throughout secondary school. Upon graduating high school, Browne matriculated at Oakwood University in Huntsville, Alabama. However, she transferred and received a Bachelor of Arts degree from Boston University.

Browne, who has been an elementary school teacher with the Virgin Islands Department of Education, has been a Choral Director at the Seventh Day Adventist Church in Peters Rest, Choral Director at Seventh Day Adventist School in Holgers Hope, Christiansted, and an accompanist for the Saint Croix Central High School Mixed Choir and Chamber Ensemble in Kingshill. In addition, Barbara-Gene Forde Browne has also been the accompanist for the Caribbean Chorale on Saint Thomas. In 2021, she performed as a vocalist with the Ladies Trio at the "Resilience:

Mobilizing for Transformation for the University of the Southern Caribbean Alumni Association" in WashingtonDC.

Sources:

Barbara-Gene Browne, The Life of K. E. Forde." Caribbean Union Gleanings, Third Quarter, 2011;

"The Caribbean Chorale's Spring Concert to Celebrate God, America and the V.I.," https://stthomassource.com/content/2005/05/21/caribbean-chorales-spring-concert-celebrate-god-america/.

"Resilience: Mobilizing for Transformation for the University of the Southern Caribbean Alumni Association,"https://uscalumnidc.org/wp-content/uploads/2021/04/Weekend-Program-Booklet.2021..pdf

Paula Harrell

Image Ownership: Fair Usage

Paula Harrell was born and reared in Durham, North Carolina, to John D. Harrell, Jr., a former math professor at North Carolina Central University, and her mother was a singer. Paula began playing the piano when she was four years old.[134]

Harrell is a graduate of North Carolina Central University. She earned a Master of Music degree in Church Music and Organ Performance from Ohio State University in Columbus in 1977. She received a Doctor of Musical Arts

---

[134] "NCCU's Music chair makes a career out of love for music," https://www.tapatalk.com/groups/nccueagles/nccu-s-music-chair-makes-a-career-out-of-love-for--t3035.html.

in Organ Performance from the University of North Carolina at Greensboro in 1992.[135]

Harrell has taught piano at North Carolina A & T State University in Greensboro and in 2004, Harrell became the chair of the Music Department at North Carolina Central University.[136]

In 2016, Dr. Paula Harrell performed the "Improvisation on We Shall Overcome," arranged by Dr. Carl Haywood at the Southeastern Regional Conference of the National Association of Negro Musicians (NANM) that took place

---

[135] "NCCU's Music chair makes a career out of love for music," https://www.tapatalk.com/groups/nccueagles/nccu-s-music-chair-makes-a-career-out-of-love-for--t3035.html.
[136] NCCU Eagles Fan Forum! Brief History of the University Band and Band Directors," https://www.tapatalk.com/groups/nccueagles/brief-history-of-the-university-band-and-band-dire-t5918.html.

in the Organ Recital Hall of the University of North Carolina at Greensboro. [137]

Sources:

Dr. Paula Harrell, Organist," https://www.youtube.com/watch?v=7Nj-6GjlH20.

"NCCU's Music chair makes a career out of love for music," https://www.tapatalk.com/groups/nccueagles/nccu-s-music-chair-makes-a-career-out-of-love-for--t3035.html.

NCCU Eagles Fan Forum! Brief History of the University Band and Band Directors," https://www.tapatalk.com/groups/nccueagles/brief-history-of-the-university-band-and-band-dire-t5918.html.

---

[137] "Dr. Paula Harrell, Organist," https://www.youtube.com/watch?v=7Nj-6GjlH20.

Part III: **COMPOSERS**

Florence Beatrice Smith Price (1887-1953)

Image Ownership: Fair Usage
Photograph by Thomas Yenser

Florence Beatrice Smith Price was born on April 9, 1887, in Little Rock, Arkansas, to James H. Smith, a dentist, and Florence Gulliver smith, a music teacher. Florence performed her first full piano recital at four. And by the time she was 11, she had completed her first orchestra composition. She studied organ, piano, and composition at the New England Conservatory of Music in Back Bay, Boston, Massachusetts, graduating in 1906. She composed over 300 works: four symphonies, and four concertos.

In 1933, Price became the first black woman composer to have a symphony performed by a major American orchestra when her Symphony No. 1 in E minor was performed by the Chicago Symphony Orchestra.[138]

Price taught music at Shorter College in Little Rock and was chairperson of the Music Department at Clark College now Clark-Atlanta University in Atlanta, Georgia.[139]
Florence Beatrice Smith Price died on June 3, 1953. She was 66.

Sources:

"About Florence B. Price," https://www.florencepricecelebration.com/about-florence-price.

"Florence Price," https://www.aso.org/composer/detail/florence-price.

---

[138] "Florence Price," https://www.aso.org/composer/detail/florence-price.
[139] "About Florence B. Price," https://www.florencepricecelebration.com/about-florence-price.

Arthur Petersen

Undine Smith Moore (1904-1989)

Image Ownership: Fair Usage

Undine Eliza Anna Smith Moore, also known as the "Dean of Black Women Composers,"[140] was born on August 24, 1904, in Jarratt, Virginia, to James William Smith and Hardie Turnbull Smith. However, she grew up in Petersburg, Virginia.[141]

At an early age, Moore began studying the piano. After high school, she enrolled in Fisk University in Nashville, Tennessee majoring in piano and organ. She graduated in

---

[140] "Undine Smith Moore," https://www.musicbyblackcomposers.org/2017/08/25/undine-smith-moore/.
[141] "Undine Smith Moore, 1904-1989," https://www.musicbywomen.org/composer/undine-smith-moore/.

1926 and soon after became the supervisor of music for the Goldsboro, North Carolina Public School System.[142]

In 1931, she earned a Master of Arts and a professional diploma in music from Teachers College of Columbia University. Afterward, Moore continued studying composition at the Manhattan School of Music, Julliard School, and the Eastman School of Music at the University of Rochester. [143]
Moore began her higher education career in music in 1927. She taught piano, theory, and composition there and was the University Organist.

In 1938, Undine Smith married Dr. James Arthur Moore, the chair of the physical education department at Virginia State College and a trained singer. They performed together and parented a daughter, Marie Hardie Moore.[144]

From 1969 to 1972, Moore was a co-founder and co-director the Black Music Center at Virginia State University. In addition, she was the recipient of a plethora of accolades, including an honorary doctorate from Virginia State University in 1972 and Indiana University in Bloomington, Indiana in 1976.[145] The next year in 1977, Moore named Music Laureate of Virginia.[146] And in 1981,

---

[142] "Undine Smith Moore," https://www.musicbyblackcomposers.org/2017/08/25/undine-smith-moore/.
[143] "Undine Smith Moore, 1904-1989," https://www.musicbywomen.org/composer/undine-smith-moore/
[144] "Undine Smith Moore," https://www.liquisearch.com/undine_smith_moore.
[145] "Undine Moore, Composer, and Teacher born," https://aaregistry.org/story/undine-moore-composer-of-note-and-innovative-music-teacher/.
[146] "Undine Smith Moore," https://www.liquisearch.com/undine_smith_moore.

Moore's Pulitzer Prize-nominated oratorio Scenes from the Life of a Martyr premiered at Carnegie Hall in New York.[147]

Undine Eliza Anna Smith Moore February 6, 1989. She was 84

Sources:

"Undine Smith Moore, 1904-1989," https://www.musicbywomen.org/composer/undine-smith-moore/;

"Undine Moore, Composer, and Teacher born," https://aaregistry.org/story/undine-moore-composer-of-note-and-innovative-music-teacher/.

---

[147] "Undine Smith Moore," https://www.musicbyblackcomposers.org/2017/08/25/undine-smith-moore/.

I Paved the Way

Tania Justina León (1945-)

Image Ownership: Fair Usage

Tania Justina León was born on May 14, 1943, in Havana, Cuba, to Oscar León and Dora Ferran León. She began studying the piano at the age of four. She received a Bachelor of Music in Piano and Theory from the Peyrellade Conservatory Music in Havana in 1963, a Master of Arts in Music Education from National Conservatory Music, Havana, in 1965, and a Bachelor of Science in Accounting from the University Havana in 1965.[148]

In 1967, León left Cuba for New York City and continued at New York University, thus receiving a Bachelor of Science in Music Education in 1973 and a Master of Arts in Composition in 1975.

---

[148] "Tania Justina León," https://prabook.com/web/tania_justina.leon/1679167.

León has held noteworthy music professorships at Brooklyn College Conservatory of Music, Yale University, and Harvard University.[149]

In 1998, she was awarded the New York Governor's Lifetime Achievement Award. And received honorary doctorates from Colgate University and Oberlin Conservatory of Music,[150] SUNY Purchase College, and the Curtis Institute of Music.[151]

In 2021, León's orchestral work Stride, was commissioned by the New York Philharmonic and was awarded the 2021 Pulitzer Prize in Music. The following year, 2022, The John F. Kennedy Center for the Performing Arts selected Tania León as one of the 45th Honorees for lifetime artistic achievements.[152]

Sources:

"Tania León," https://www.windrep.org/Tania_Leon;

"Tania Justina León," https://prabook.com/web/tania_justina.leon/1679167.

---

[149] "Tania Justina León," https://prabook.com/web/tania_justina.leon/1679167.
[150] "Tania León," https://www.windrep.org/Tania_Leon.
[151] "Tania León," https://www.kennedy-center.org/.
[152] "Tania León," https://www.kennedy-center.org/.

Nkeiru Okoye (1972-)

Image Ownership: Fair Usage

Nkeiru Okoye was born on July 18, 1972, and was reared in New York to an Igbo father from Nigeria and an African American mother. Nkeiru began piano studies at eight; five years later, at 13, she was composing.

Okoye attended the Preparatory Division of the Manhattan School of Music and received a Bachelor of Music degree from Oberlin Conservatory of Music in Oberlin, Ohio, where she studied composition, music theory, piano, conducting, and Africana Studies.[153] She earned a Doctor of

---

[153] "Nkeiru Okoye," https://www.nkeiruokoye.com/bio.

Philosophy degree in Music Theory and Composition from Rutgers University.[154]

Okoye's opera *Harriet Tubman: When I Crossed That Line to Freedom* was premiered by American Opera Projects with support from The National Endowment of the Arts. 2014.

In 2017, Okoye completed *Invitation to a Die-In* (in memory of Trayvon Martin) was commissioned and premiered by conductor Ng Tian Hui and the Mount Holyoke Symphony Orchestra.

The following year in 2018, Okoye was commissioned to compose an orchestral work for the 250th anniversary of the founding of Charlotte, North Carolina, Charlotte Symphony Orchestra.

In 2020, *the opera Black Bottom* by Okoye was completed. It was performed and conducted by Thomas Wilkens and the Detroit Symphony Orchestra in 2021 in celebration of the Symphony Hall Centennial. She is a 2021 Guggenheim Fellow in music composition.[155]

Sources:

"Nkeiru Okoye," https://www.nkeiruokoye.com/bio.

"Nkeiru Okoye," https://www.theprimaveraproject.com/composer/nkeiru-okoye/.

---

[154] "Nkeiru Okoye," https://www.theprimaveraproject.com/composer/nkeiru-okoye/.
[155] "SSC Transform 2021 commissioned composer: Dr. Nkeiru Okoye," https://sscmusic.org/nkeiru-okoye/.

"SSC Transform 2021 commissioned composer: Dr. Nkeiru Okoye," https://sscmusic.org/nkeiru-okoye/.

Arthur Petersen
SELECTED MUSIC PROGRAMS

Curtis Institute of Music (the most competitive in the United States)
Philadelphia, Pennsylvania

Instituto Superior de Arte, Facultad de Musica
Havana, Cuba

Oberlin Conservatory of Music (oldest conservatory in the United States)
Oberlin, Ohio

Howard University Department of Music
Washington, DC

University of Cincinnati College Conservatory of Music
Cincinnati, Ohio

Juilliard School
New York, New York

Royal Conservatory of Music
Toronto, Ontario, Canada

L'école de musique Vincent-d'Indy
Montreal, Quebec, Canada

Manhattan School of Music
New York, New York

Oakwood University Department of Music
Huntsville, Alabama

Berklee College of Music
Boston, Massachusetts

I Paved the Way

Florida A & M University School of Music
Tallahassee, Florida

Mannes College-The New School for Music
New York, New York

Morgan State University School of Music
Baltimore, Maryland
New England Conservatory of Music
Boston, Massachusetts

Boston Conservatory
Boston, Massachusetts

Cleveland Institute of Music
Cleveland, Ohio

Conservatorio de Música de Puerto Rico
San Juan, Puerto Rico

San Francisco Conservatory of Music
San Francisco, California

Northern Caribbean University
Music Building, Mandeville, Jamaica

Johns Hopkins University Peabody Conservatory of Music
Baltimore, Maryland

University of Rochester Eastman School of Music
Rochester, New York

Academy of Vocal Arts
Philadelphia, Pennsylvania

Indiana University Jacobs School of Music
Bloomington, Indiana

Arthur Petersen
University of Michigan School of Music, Theatre & Dance
Ann Arbor, Michigan

Los Angeles College of Music
Pasadena, California

McNally Smith College of Music
Saint Paul, Minnesota

Musicians Institute
Los Angeles, California

I Paved the Way
SELECTED OPERA HOUSES IN YOUR AREA

Abraham Chavez Theatre, El Paso, Texas

Academy of Music, Philadelphia, Pennsylvania

Alexandria Opera House, Alexandria, Egypt

Ankara Opera House, Ankara, Turkey

Artscape Opera House, Cape Town, South Africa

Bass Performance Hall, Fort Worth, Texas

Benedum Center, Pittsburgh, Pennsylvania

Bolshoi, Moscow, Russia

Boston Opera House, Boston, Massachusetts

Brooklyn Academy of Music, Brooklyn, New York

Cairo Opera House, Cairo, Egypt

California Theater, San Jose, California

Carpenter Theater, Richmond, Virginia

Casa da Música, Porto, Portugal

Central City Opera House, Central City, Colorado

Centro de Bellas Artes Luis A. Ferré, Santurce, Puerto Rico

Chamber Opera House, Chicago, Illinois

Chicago Opera House, Chicago, Illinois

Civic Opera House, Chicago, Illinois

Copenhagen Opera House, Copenhagen, Denmark

Crosby's Opera House, Chicago, Illinois

Dofasco Centre for the Performing Arts, Hamilton, Ontario

Dubai Opera, Dubai, United Arab Emirates

Elgin Theatre, Opera Atelier, Toronto, Ontario

Estates Theater, Prague, Poland

Golda Center for Performing Arts, Tel Aviv, Israel

Gran Teatro de la Habana, Havana, Cuba

Gran Teatro del Cibao, Santiago, Dominican Republic

Gran Teatro Nacional, México City, México

Grand Opera House, Chicago, Illinois

Guangzhou Opera House, Guangzhou, China

Harrison Opera House, Norfolk, Virginia

Hungarian State Opera House, Budapest, Hungary

Island Center for the Performing Arts, Christiansted, Virgin Islands

La Scala, Milan, Italy

Margravial Opera House, Bayreuth, Germany

Mariinsky Theater, Saint Petersburg, Russia

Metropolitan Opera, New York, New York

National Theatre Munich, Munich, Germany

I Paved the Way

Opera de Monte-Carlo, Monaco

Opéra Royal de Versailles, Versailles, France

Paris Opéra, Paris, France

Queen Elizabeth Theatre, Vancouver, British Columbia

Reichhold Center for the Arts, Charlotte Amalie, Virgin Islands

Royal Opera House, London, England

Royal Opera House, Mumbai, India

Royal Opera House, Stockholm, Sweden

Royal Theatre, Victoria, British Columbia

Sydney Opera House, Sydney, Australia

Stavros Niarchos Foundation Cultural Center, Athens, Greece

Teatro Colón, Buenos Aires, Argentina

Teatro La Fenice, Venice, Italy

Teatro La Perla, Ponce, Puerto Rico

Teatro Massimo, Palermo, Italy

Teatro di San Carlo, Naples, Italy

Teatro Tapia, Old San Juan, Puerto Rico

Théâtre municipal de Casablanca, Morocco

Vienna Staatsoper/Vienna State Opera House, Vienna, Austria

Winspear Opera House, Dallas, Texas

Ziff Ballet Opera House, Miami, Florida

NOTES

"About Florence B. Price," https://www.florencepricecelebration.com/about-florence-price.

Adam Bernstein, "Charlotte Holloman, concert singer and voice teacher, dies at 93," https://www.washingtonpost.com/people/adam-bernstein/.

"Adele Addison," https://wbssmedia.com/artists/detail/1667.

"Adele Addison, Opera Vocalist, born," https://aaregistry.org/story/adelle-addison-one-of-o.

"Adele Allen," https://www.linkedin.com/in/adele-allen-m-d-42b77614/;

"Adele's World of Music: Classical and Modern Music," https://adelesworldofmusic.webs.com/.

Alex Ross, "Black Scholars Confront White Supremacy in Classical Music," https://www.newyorker.com/magazine/2020/09/21/black-scholars-confront-white-supremacy-in-classical-music.

"All About Ella Ruth Lee Biography: Career, Family, Songs, and Death," https://howafrica.com/all-about-ella-ruth-lee-biography-career-family-songs-and-death/.

Allan Keiler, "Marian Anderson: A Singer's Journey," https://archive.nytimes.com/www.nytimes.com/books/first/k/keiler-anderson.html.

"Alphonso Forbes," https://www.ancientfaces.com/person/alphonso-forbes-birth-1895-death-1976/90968841.

"Alumna Angel Joy Blue returns to UCLA to perform on Nov. 21," https://newsroom.ucla.edu/releases/alumna-angel-joy-blue-returns-to-ucla-to-perform-on-nov-21;

Amir Vera and Pierre Meilhan, "Jessye Norman, international opera star, dead at 74," https://www.cnn.com/2019/09/30/entertainment/jessye-norman-obit/index.html;

"Angel Blue," https://www.angeljoyblue.com/?q=AboutAngel.

"Angel Joy Blue," https://www.imdb.com/name/nm7554879/bio.

Anne Midgette, "From rising star to grande dame, Martina Arroyo never forgot who she was," https://www.washingtonpost.com/entertainment/music/from-rising-star-to-grande-dame-martina-arroyo-never-forgot-who-she-was/2013/12/05/39958edc-5798-11e3-835d-e7173847c7cc_story.html.

Ashawnta Jackson, "The Life of Matilda Sissieretta Jones," https://daily.jstor.org/the-life-of-matilda-sissieretta-jones.

"Audra McDonald, Tony & Grammy Award Winner, Visits Saint Mary's College," https://www.saintmarys.edu/news-events/news-releases/audra-mcdonald-margaret-hill-visiting-artist-2013.

Barbara-Gene Browne, The Life of K. E. Forde." Caribbean Union Gleanings, Third Quarter, 2011.

Biografías y Vidas, "Cirilo Villaverde," https://www.biografiasyvidas.com/biografia/v/villaverde.htm;

"The Caribbean Chorale's Spring Concert to Celebrate God, America and the V.I.,"https://stthomassource.com/content/2005/05/21/caribbean-chorales-spring-concert-celebrate-god-america/.

"Carmen Velma Shepperd Explained," https://everything.explained.today/Carmen_Velma_Shepperd/.

"Camilla Williams," https://www.danvillemuseum.org/content/uploads/PDF/exhibits/camilla/camilla_book_cover.pdf.

David Salazar, "From Refugee To Mimì – Soprano Elizabeth Caballero On Her Journey From Cuban Outcast to Opera Star," https://operawire.com/from-refugee-to-mimi-soprano-elizabeth-caballero-on-her-journey-from-cuban-outcast-to-opera-star/;

"Dorothy Maynor Biography," https://afrovoices.com/dorothy-maynor-biography/.

"Edwards, Pearly Hayslett, Geraldine Hayslett Boone, and Jeanette Wallace, 1980, 1995," https://archives.lib.duke.edu/catalog/behindtheveil_aspace_1102fddb-2c64-4077-8455-604e2f0a6008;

" Elizabeth Caballero, Soprano," https://venetianartssociety.org/events/elizabeth-caballero-soprano/;

"Elizabeth Taylor Greenfield," https://www.nps.gov/people/elizabeth-taylor-greenfield.htm.

"Elizabeth Taylor Greenfield," https://www.thoughtco.com/elizabeth-taylor-greenfield-biography-45259.

"Ella Ruth Lee Romani (1933-2013)," blacknewszone.com › ella-ruth-lee-romani-1933-2013.

Erika Weber, "Charlotte Wesley Holloman," https://www.blackpast.org/african-american-history/holloman-charlotte-wesley-1922-2015/.

Eva Cahen, "Sitting down with Angel Joy Blue," http://www.operavivra.com/articles/interviews/sitting-down-with-angel-joy-blue/;

"Everett Lee, First African-American to Conduct on Broadway, Has Died at 105," https://theviolinchannel.com/everett-lee-the-first-african-american-to-conduct-on-broadway-has-died-aged-105/.

"Florence Price," https://www.aso.org/composer/detail/florence-price.
Fred Plotkin, "Discovering Charlotte Wesley Holloman," https://www.wqxr.org/story/discovering-charlotte-wesley-holloman/.

"Grace Bumbry," https://musicianguide.com/biographies/1608000604/Grace-Bumbry.html.

"Grace Bumbry," https://gracebumbry.com/biography/.

Grammy Awards, "Angel Blue," https://www.grammy.com/artists/angel-blue/287143.

"Harlem's Dorothy Maynor Harlem School Of The Arts Founder And A Woman Of Many Firsts," https://www.harlemworldmagazine.com/harlems-dorothy-maynor-harlem-school-of-the-arts-founder-and-a-woman-of-many-firsts/.

"Hazel Scott," https://www.womenshistory.org/education-resources/biographies/hazel-scott;

"Hazel Scott," https://www.smithsonianmag.com/arts-culture/hazel-scotts-lifetime-of-high-notes-145939027/;

"Her Story: Nina Simone,"http://shemadehistory.com/her-story-nina-simone/;

"Hildred E. Roach," https://www.officialusa.com/names/Hildred-Roach.

"Hunter Congratulates Opera Singer Martina Arroyo '56, Recipient of the 2013 Kennedy Center Honors," https://www.hunter.cuny.edu/communications/pressroom/news/hunter-congratulates-opera-singer-martina-arroyo-201956-2013-recipient-of-the-kennedy-center-honors.

"In the Park with Elizabeth Caballero," https://www.madisonopera.org/2018/07/06/in-the-park-with-elizabeth-caballero/;

"Ingrid A. Bough, JD," https://outskirtspress.com/violetlovestheletterv.

Interviews, Editorials, Humour, Reviews, How-to Op Eds News," https://www.schmopera.com/talking-with-singers-elizabeth-caballero/;

"James L. Stafford," https://www.legacy.com/us/obituaries/washingtonpost/name/james-stafford-obituary?id=5514046.

"Jessye Norman," https://thedig.howard.edu/featured-people/jessye-norman.

Judi Shimel, "Friends and Family Reflect on Lorraine Baa's Life and Legacy," https://stcroixsource.com/2021/11/02/friends-and-family-reflect-on-lorraine-baas-life-and-legacy/.

Karla Rixon, "Mattiwilda Dobbs," https://www.blackpast.org/african-american-history/dobbs-mattiwilda-1925/.

"Kathleen Battle's Awards, "https://m.imdb.com/name/nm0061513/awards.

"Kathleen Battle,"https://www.u-s-history.com/pages/h3854.html.
"Leontyne Price," http://awardsandwinners.com/winner/?mid=/m/025027.

"Leontyne Price, Legendary Diva, Is a Movie Star at 90," https://www.nytimes.com/2017/12/22/arts/music/leontyne-price-met-opera.html.

Linnea Crowther, "Jessye Norman (1945–2019), Grammy-winning opera singer," https://www.legacy.com/news/celebrity-deaths/jessye-norman-1945-2019-grammy-winning-opera-singer/.

Lisa Torem, "Nina Simone - Nina Simone," https://pennyblackmusic.co.uk/Home/DetailsMobile?id=21081.

"Lorraine E. Baa," https://inforver.com/view/Lorraine-Baa-C5DNBd.

Lucien H. White, "Carmen Velma Shepperd Graduates in Singing from Damrosch Institute," https://www.newspapers.com/clip/72178121/carmen-velma-shepperd-graduates.

Maddy Shaw Roberts, "Who was Hazel Scott, the forgotten jazz virtuoso who fought against racial segregation?" https://amp.classicfm.com/discover-music/instruments/piano/hazel-scott-jazz-entertainer-fought-racial-segregation/;

Margalit Fox, "Camilla Williams, Barrier-Breaking Opera Star, Dies at 92," https://www.nytimes.com/2012/02/03/arts/music/camilla-williams-opera-singer-dies-at-92.html.

Margalit Fox, "Mattiwilda Dobbs, Soprano and Principal at Met, Dies at 90," https://www.nytimes.com/2015/12/11/arts/music/mattiwilda-dobbs-black-soprano-and-principal-at-met-dies-at-90.html.

Mariana Brandman, "Nina Simone," https://www.ninasimone.com/biography/;
"Martina Arroya," https://www.kennedy-center.org/artists/a/ao-az/martina-arroyo/.

" Matilda Sissieretta Joyner Jones," http://riheritagehalloffame.com/matilda-sissieretta-joyner-jones/.

"Mattiwilda Dobbs," https://samepassage.org/mattiwilda-dobbs/.

"Marian Anderson,' http://marian-anderson.com/biography/.

"Marian Anderson," https://www.imdb.com/name/nm0993450/bio.

The Metropolitan Opera, " Elizabeth Caballero, Soprano," https://www.metopera.org/discover/artists/soprano/elizabeth-caballero/.

"Mezzo-Soprano Muriel Burrell Smith (1923-1985)," https://wap.org.ng/read/mezzo-soprano-muriel-burrell-smith-1923-1985/.

"Muriel Burrell Smith," https://www.encyclopedia.com/women/dictionaries-thesauruses-pictures-and-press-releases/smith-muriel-burrell-1923-1985.

"Muriel Burrell Smith Dies," https://www.washingtonpost.com/archive/local/1985/09/16/muriel-burrell-smith-dies/a6ce61f9-ac81-494c-8d67-84f188bb9a3e/.

New Journal & Guide, "Social And Civic Whirl: Mrs. Geraldine T. Boone Receives The Roland Carter Living Legends In Church Music Honor," https://thenewjournalandguide.com/social-civic-whirl-mrs-geraldine-t-boone-receives-roland-carter-living-legends-church-music-honor/.

"Nina Simone's 'Lovely, Precious Dream' For Black Children," https://www.npr.org/2019/01/08/683021559/nina-simone-to-be-young-gifted-and-black-american-anthem.

"Nkeiru Okoye," https://www.nkeiruokoye.com/bio.

"Nkeiru Okoye," https://www.theprimaveraproject.com/composer/nkeiru-okoye/.

"Omo Bello Musical Journey And Life In Brief," https://phamoxmusic.com/omo-bello/.

"Omo Bello Musical Journey And Life In Brief," https://phamoxmusic.com/omo-bello/.

"Omo Bello," http://www.omobello.com/about.html.

"On Island Profile: Ingrid A. Bough," https://stcroixsource.com/2006/01/10/island-profile-ingrid-bough/.

"On Island Profile: Onika Michelle Thomas," https://stthomassource.com/content/2005/07/13/island-profile-onika-michelle-thomas/;

"Orlando Baa," https://www.myheritage.com/names/orlando_baa.

Otis Alexander, "Adele Addison Berger," https://www.blackpast.org/african-american-history/people-african-american-history/adele-addison-berger-1925/.

Otis D Alexander, *One Drop of Imagination: Embracing Selected Arts Energies* (New York: African Tree Press, 2019).

Part of the Singers on Singing: Signature Roles series, " Singers on Singing: Grace Bumbry discusses Amneris," https://hampsongfoundation.org/resource/singers-on-singing-grace-bumbry-discusses-amneris/.

"President's Corner: President Lorraine E. Baa," https://portal.clubrunner.ca/1579/Stories/president-s-corner-president-lorraine-e.-baa.

"Resilience: Mobilizing for Transformation for the University of the Southern Caribbean Alumni Association," https://uscalumnidc.org/wp-content/uploads/2021/04/Weekend-Program-Booklet.2021.pdf.

Robert Viagas, "Grammy Winner Will Succeed Audra McDonald in Shuffle Along; Savion Glover Joining the Cast," https://www.playbill.com/article/grammy-winner-will-succeed-audra-mcdonald-in-shuffle-along-savion-glover-joining-the-cast.

Ross McDonagh, "Heavily pregnant Audra McDonald, 46, receives National Medal of Arts - and a warm hug - from President Obama," https://www.dailymail.co.uk/tvshowbiz/article-3802670/Audra-McDonald-receives-National-Medal-Arts-warm-hug-President-Obama.html.

"Spinto Soprano Martina Arroyo," https://www.martinaarroyo.com/.

"Sylvia Lee: Coach, Master," https://prabook.com/web/sylvia.lee/1836410.

"Tania León," https://www.windrep.org/Tania_Leon.

"Tania Justina León," https://prabook.com/web/tania_justina.leon/1679167.

"Tribute to Sylvia Olden Lee, Master Musician and Teacher,"

https://larouchepub.com/other/2017/4426tribute_sylvia.html.

"Undine Smith Moore," https://www.musicbyblackcomposers.org/2017/08/25/undine-smith-moore/.

" Undine Smith Moore, 1904-1989," https://www.musicbywomen.org/composer/undine-smith-moore/.

"Undine Smith Moore, 1904-1989," https://www.musicbywomen.org/composer/undine-smith-moore/
"Undine Moore, Composer, and Teacher born," https://aaregistry.org/story/undine-moore-composer-of-note-and-innovative-music-teacher/.

"University of Pennsylvania, Honorary Degree Recipients," https://secretary.upenn.edu/ceremonies/honorary-degree-recipients/alphabetical/n.

"Who's Hazel Scott? (Unsung Women of Jazz #11)," https://curtjazz.com/2019/02/20/whos-hazel-scott-unsung-women-of-jazz-11-2/.

BIBLIOGRAPHY

Abdul, Raoul. *Blacks in Classical Music: A Personal History*. New York: Dodd, Mead & Company, 1977.

Alexander, Otis D. *Proper Ladies: Selected African American/Women of Color in the Fine & Lively Arts*. Astoria, NY: African Tree Press, 2017.

Alexander, Otis D. *Classical Music, Racism, and Perceptions: A Reference Source for Recounting of African-American Pioneers and Contemporaries*. Astoria, NY: African Tree Press, 2016.

Alexander, Otis D. *One Drop of Imagination: Embracing Selected Arts Energies*. Astoria, NY: African Tree Press, 2020.

Baiocchi, Regina Harris. "Spirituals." In *Black Women in America*. Oxford University Press, 2005. https://www-oxfordreference-com.ezproxy.elon.edu/view/10.1093/acref/9780195156775.001.0001/acref-9780195156775-e-0409.

De Lerma, Dominique-René and Marsha J. Reisser. *Black Music and Musicians in the New Grove Dictionary of American Music and the New Harvard Dictionary of Music*. CBMR Monographs. Chicago: Center for Black Music Research, Columbia College, 1989.

Green, Mildred Denby. "Composers." In *Black Women in America*.: Oxford University Press, 2005. https://www-oxfordreference-com.ezproxy.elon.edu/view/10.1093/acref/9780195156775.001.0001/acref-9780195156775-e-0089.

Harris, Carl, and Undine Smith Moore. "Composer and Master Teacher." *The Black Perspective in Music* 13, no. 1 (1985): 79-90. Accessed June 16, 2021. doi:10.2307/1214794.

Horowitz, Joseph. *Dvořák's Prophesy: And the Vexed Fate of Black Classical* Music. New York, W.W. Norton & Company, 2021.

Hutchinson, Earl Ofari. *It's Our Music Too: The Black Experience in Classical Music*. Los Angeles: Middle Passage Press, 2016.

Mattis, Olivia. "Moore, Undine Smith." *Grove Music Online.* January 20, 2001. https://doi.org/10.1093/gmo/9781561592630.article.47040.

"Moore, Undine Smith." *Harvard Biographical Dictionary of Music*, June 1996, 606. http://search.ebscohost.com.ezproxy.elon.edu/login.aspx?direct=true&db=b6h&AN=36201660&site=brc-live.

"Notable Virginia Women – Undine Smith (1904-1989)." *Working Out Her Destiny: Women's History in Virginia, 1600-2004*." Accessed August 6, 2021. https://www.lva.virginia.gov/exhibits/destiny/notable/smith.htm.

Phillip Jr., Cipriani A. *Storytelling, Storytellers & Information Systems: with Emphasis on the Virgin Islands*. New York: Masa Books, 2022.

Southern, Eileen. *The Music of Black Americans: A History*. 3rd ed. New York, W.W. Norton & Company, 1997.

Roach, Hildred. *Black American Music: Past and Present: Pan-African Composers Thenceforth and Now*

Smith, Eric Ledell. *Blacks in Opera: An Encyclopedia of People and Companies, 1873-1993*. McFarland Publishing, 1995.

Southern, Eileen and Josephine Wright. *Images: Iconography of Music in African American Culture (1770s-1920s)*. Garland Reference Library of the Humanities Volume 1. New York: Routledge, 2000.

Stewart, James. "Timeline: Undine Smith Moore (1904-1989)." *Vermont Public Radio*. March 22, 2021. https://www.vpr.org/programs/2021-03-22/timeline-undine-smith-moore-1904-1989.

www.ingramcontent.com/pod-product-compliance
Lightning Source LLC
Chambersburg PA
CBHW051939160426
43198CB00013B/2219